The God Who Sits Enthroned

Evidence for God's Existence

Phil Fernandes

Xulon Press
11350 Random Hills Road
Suite 800
Fairfax, VA 22030
(703) 279-6511
XulonPress.com

To order additional copies, call 1-866-909-BOOK (2665).

With all my love,
to my wife Cathy,
my best friend next to Jesus.

Acknowledgments

I am forever grateful for the efforts of those who aided me in the completion of this book. Dr. Rick Walston of Faraston Theological Seminary and Eric Purcell of the Institute of Biblical Defense both read the manuscript and made helpful suggestions. I appreciate the IBD research staff. They have sharpened my argumentation through hours of discussion (Proverbs 27:17). Without the encouragement and support of the Claytons, the Streutkers, and the Rinears, this present work would still be a dream. I praise God that He blessed me with a father, Joseph Fernandes, who set a noble example for me by studying the writings of Augustine and Aquinas long before I even knew Jesus. I am also thankful for the diligent study and writings of the leading Christian apologists who have influenced my thought. They include Gary Habermas, J. P. Moreland, William Lane Craig, and Norman Geisler. And, finally, I will always appreciate the love, patience, and encouragement of my wife Cathy.

Table of Contents

Introduction

═══════════════════════

Does God Exist? Were we created by a personal, rational God who designed us for a purpose? Or, is the universe, man included, merely a product of chance—a random throwing together of molecules? Does life have meaning? Are there such things as right and wrong? Will there be life after death and a future judgment? The question of God's existence, since it touches on issues of meaning, morality, and life after death, is of utmost importance.

This book provides the reader with evidence for the existence of the God of the Bible. The Bible teaches that there is only one true God, and that He is the Creator of all else that exists. The Scriptures declare God to be an eternal, all-knowing personal Being who is both transcendent (separate from His creation) and immanent (involved with His creation). This biblical view of God is called theism, and it is this concept of God that this book attempts to defend.

Apologetics is the defense of the Christian Faith. This book utilizes three different types of apologetic methodologies.

Part One of this book provides the reader with psychological evidence for God's existence. Psychological apologetics appeals to the emotions and will of man, attempting to persuade him to choose the God of the Bible rather than the undesirable alternative of life without God.

Part Two examines the field of philosophical apologetics (also known as philosophy of religion) by providing rational arguments for the existence of the God of the Bible. This section critiques the world views which oppose theism, discusses the traditional arguments for God's existence, and proposes solutions to the problems of evil, miracles, and moral relativism.

Part Three concludes this book with a brief discussion of scientific apologetics. This section discusses the scientific case for creation and as well as scientific evidences against evolution.

PART ONE

Psychological
Apologetics

CHAPTER 1

The Absurdity of Life Without God

P sychological Apologetics attempts to deal with the whole man, not just his reason. The will and emotions of man are taken into account. Man desperately needs meaning in life, and apologists who use this methodology often focus on this fact. They point out that if there is no God, then life is absurd and without ultimate meaning.

Psychological apologists also focus on man's innate thirst to transcend this earthly experience (chapter 2), and the paradox of man—that man is both wonderful and cruel (chapter 3). An adequate world view must offer a viable explanation for these three phenomena (the absurdity of life without God, the thirst for transcendence, and the paradox of man). Psychological apologists argue that Christianity provides a better answer in these areas than any other world view.

KING SOLOMON

This chapter will examine the argument for God's existence based on the absurdity of life without God. Though this argument is popular today, it is not new. In fact, King Solomon of Israel used this argument as far back as 935 BC. This is interesting in light of the fact that most historians place the start of philosophy at about 585 BC.[1] However, there were wise thinkers at a much earlier time. As Solomon began his reign, he prayed for wisdom and knowledge (2 Chronicles 1:10-12). God answered his prayer and his wisdom surpassed that of all other men of his day. People came from remote parts of the earth just to ask him "difficult questions" (1 Kings 4:29-34). The biblical account of Solomon's wisdom is as follows:

> Now God gave Solomon wisdom and very great discernment and breadth of mind, like the sand that is on the seashore. And Solomon's wisdom surpassed the wisdom of all the sons of the east and all the wisdom of Egypt. For he was wiser than all men, than Ethan the Ezrahite, Heman, Calcol and Darda, the sons of Mahol; and his fame was known in all the surrounding nations. He also spoke 3,000 proverbs, and his songs were 1,005. And he spoke of trees, from the cedar that is in Lebanon even to the hyssop that grows on the wall; he spoke also of animals and birds and creeping things and fish. And men came from all peoples to hear the wisdom of Solomon, from all

the kings of the earth who had heard of his wisdom (1 Kings 4:29-34).

Solomon's two philosophical writings are *Proverbs* and *Ecclesiastes*. In *Proverbs*, Solomon teaches wisdom that can be applied to daily life. It can be viewed as a manual on practical living. In Ecclesiastes, Solomon shows that a man's life is totally meaningless until he recognizes his relation to God.

Solomon begins his work sounding like a modern-day existentialist. He cries, "Vanity of vanities! All is vanity" (Ecclesiastes 1:2). He expresses the view that life is futile and that man is thrust into a state of deep despair. However, Solomon makes this bleak assessment of human existence only when he considers the human condition "under the sun" (1:9). Solomon is attempting to find purpose in life without any appeal to man's relation to God. Solomon says that if you take the God of heaven out of the equation, life has no meaning. Man, viewed strictly from an earthly perspective, has no hope or purpose.

Solomon proclaims that ". . . in much wisdom there is much grief, and increasing knowledge results in increasing pain" (1:18). The human situation is such that the more that is known of it, the less hope there is (so long as man is viewed in isolation from God).

Solomon attempts to find meaning and purpose in life apart from God. He finds none. Apart from God, life is futile. Solomon surveys a list of candidates that might bring meaning to life apart from God. But he finds in them only frustration and "striving after the wind" (1:14). The attainment of human wisdom is vain (1:17-18). It brings no lasting satisfaction. Laughter and pleasure-seeking are vain (2:2,10). There is no genuine satisfaction in the drinking of wine (2:3) or engaging in building projects (2:4). The accumulation of wealth is without lasting significance (2:8). Music and women can provide only temporary pleasure (2:8). Even popularity amounts to nothing (2:9). Solomon's conclusion is that "everything is futility and striving after the wind" (2:17).

Though Solomon grieves for all that is "under the sun," he also begins to acknowledge God's purposes in the affairs of this world (3:1-11). He states that God has placed eternity in the hearts of men (3:11). Though man cannot fully understand the ways of God, he has an innate longing for the eternal things of God. Without appealing to these eternal matters, man will be damned to a life of despair and frustration. But if man acknowledges God and serves Him, life has meaning and eternal significance.

Solomon closes Ecclesiastes with these words. "The conclusion, when all has been heard, is: fear God and keep His commandments, because this applies to every person. For God will bring every act to judgment, everything which is hidden, whether it is good or evil" (12:13-14).

Man's search for satisfaction and meaning in life is futile if he only looks "under the sun." Life without God is useless and absurd. Despair is inevitable for all who recognize the futility found in the temporary pleasures of life. True satisfaction can only be found in God. Once man acknowledges God's existence, the works of man are no longer meaningless. What we do on earth takes on eternal significance. For we must all give an account to God for our actions. God alone gives genuine meaning to life.

Many modern thinkers have rejected the existence of God, but they also recognize that life is without meaning if there is no God. Still, they live lives of despair (or escape this despair through an existential leap) rather than submit to God who can give meaning to life. Solomon calls upon these modern thinkers to make a choice. A blind leap into the irrational realm to find meaning is not an option for honest thinkers. Man must choose God or despair. There is no other choice.

BLAISE PASCAL (1623-1662)

The Christian thinker Blaise Pascal revolted against the idea that reason alone should settle religious truth questions. Pascal realized that there is more to the decision-making processes of man than mere thought. Man's choices are also influenced by his emotions and will. "We know the truth not only through our reason but also through our heart."[2] Therefore, Pascal set out to develop a defense of the Christian Faith that appealed to these aspects in man.

Pascal stated, "Being unable to cure death, wretchedness and ignorance, men have decided, in order to be happy, not to think about such things."[3] Men "have a secret instinct driving them to seek external diversion and occupation, and this is the result of their constant sense of wretchedness."[4] ". . . it makes a man happy to be diverted from contemplating his private miseries by making him care about nothing else but dancing well . . ."[5]

Pascal saw in man a tendency to focus his attentions on

temporary pleasures rather than on his own wretched state and certain death. If a man could amuse himself with these temporary pleasures, he could ignore and deny the more important issues of life that cause him fear. But Pascal warns that there is no genuine satisfaction in this world. He says, "in this life there is no true and solid satisfaction" and that "all our pleasures are mere vanity."[6] Pascal concludes "that the only good thing in this life is the hope of another life."[7]

According to Pascal, "there are only two classes of persons who can be called reasonable: those who serve God with all their heart because they know him and those who seek him with all their heart because they do not know him."[8] Pascal considered the possibility of life after death to be of such great importance that he considered those who were not concerned about investigating this issue to be without feeling.[9] Pascal graphically describes the human situation apart from God:

> Imagine a number of men in chains, all under the sentence of death, some of whom are each day butchered in the sight of others; those remaining see their own condition in that of their fellows, and looking at each other with grief and despair await their turn. This is an image of the human condition.[10]

All men face their own inevitable death. As they go through life, they seek to hide this dreadful fact from themselves through temporary pleasures. But, as far as Pascal is concerned, this is a meaningless existence. Man can only find genuine meaning in life if he finds the God of the Bible. Apart from God, life is absurd.

Pascal calls his readers to make a choice. It is foolish for them to go on deceiving themselves. They must admit that without God and eternal life, human existence is without hope. Man must choose between despair and God. If a person wagers on God and loses, the person loses nothing. But if a person wagers on God and wins, the person wins everything. If, however, one wagers against God there is no hope of winning. If that person wins, he wins nothing. But if one bets against God and loses, he loses everything. Pascal concludes that the wise man will therefore wager on God.[11] Pascal, contrary to popular belief, is not attempting to prove God's existence with his wager argument. Instead, he is attempting to persuade others to desire and seek God with all their hearts. Pascal believed that if a person seeks God with all his heart, he will find Him (Jeremiah 29:13).

FRANCIS SCHAEFFER (1912-1984)

Christian thinker Francis Schaeffer effectively argued that life is absurd without the existence of the God of the Bible. He believed that modern man had thrust himself into a state of despair. Schaeffer saw three key philosophers as leading man away from reason and into this feeling of meaningless existence.

Immanuel Kant (1724-1804) was the first of these key thinkers. He brought secular philosophy to a halt. His thought concluded that man could only know reality as it appeared to him (phenomena) and not reality as it is (noumena). Man's mind could not bridge the gap between the two. When one begins with unaided human reason, the phenomena and noumena never meet.[12] At this point, secular philosophers gave up their attempt to find "a unified rationalistic circle that would contain all thought, and in which they could live."[13]

The next thinker emphasized by Schaeffer was Hegel (1770-1831). Before him, philosophers for thousands of years had attempted to find truth based on antithesis. This meant that they held to the idea of absolute truth. Something could not be both true and not true at the same time and in the same sense. But Kant had shown that unaided human reason within the boundaries of antithesis led to skepticism about the real world. Hegel therefore concluded that man must try a new method. He recommended abandoning absolutes. His dialectical approach allowed for the synthesizing of contradictory statements.[14] This shift in the concept of truth from antithesis (absolute truth) to synthesis (truth is relative) resulted in modern man's new way of viewing reality.[15] At this point, modern man faces great despair. For there is no longer any hope of man finding true meaning to life. There are no absolutes. Truth is relative.

The third philosopher Schaeffer discusses is Soren Kierkegaard (1813-1855). With the rejection of absolutes, modern man was left without meaning in life. Despair seemed to be the only alternative. But this is where Kierkegaard enters the scene. Schaeffer states that Kierkegaard realized that "Man has no meaning, no purpose, no significance" in the rational realm. "There is only pessimism concerning man as man." But if man takes a leap of blind faith into the nonrational realm, says Kierkegaard, this non reasonable faith gives man optimism.[16]

Schaeffer sees modern man as facing a choice between

despair and a false, nonrational hope. Schaeffer's method of evangelizing modern man is to show him that he must reason with absolutes. For the only way to deny absolutes is to assume there are absolutes.[17] The Kierkegaardian leap into the nonrational realm is therefore not an option. If the modern man refuses to turn to the God of the Bible, he is damned to a meaningless life of despair (that is, if he has enough courage to refrain from a nonrational leap). Only when a person accepts the existence of the God of the Bible can life have true meaning. Without God, life is absurd. Without God, the reasonable man will wallow in despair.

GORDON LEWIS

In his work entitled *Testing Christianity's Truth Claims*, Gordon Lewis approvingly discusses the psychological apologetics utilized by Edward John Carnell and Vernon C. Grounds. Lewis recognizes the fact that Christianity alone is able to relieve man's deepest anxieties. Science and Philosophy can offer no substitute for God's unconditional love.[18] All people long for loving acceptance, peace, and significance. Only in Jesus can these needs be met. Jesus loves each person unconditionally. He will never stop loving any individual (though each person has the freedom to reject His love and suffer the consequences). Trusting in His promises gives man peace in the midst of trials. One can find true significance in human existence only if he recognizes that all people were created by God for the purpose of eternal fellowship with Him.

Man desperately needs forgiveness to remove his guilt

and hope to obliterate his despair. But without Christ's atoning death on Calvary, there is no forgiveness. And without Christ's resurrection from the dead, there can be no genuine hope for man. Only in Christianity can man's deepest psychological needs be met.[19]

The stresses of modern life inflict multitudes with anxiety and despair. Modern man is crying out for help. Psychologists often correctly diagnose the problems, but seldom provide any real solutions. The source of man's anxiety stems from his alienation from God, and only the gospel of Jesus Christ can remedy this. The world desperately seeks joy and peace. However, joy and peace can only be found in Christ, and the church must make this known.

LAWRENCE J. CRABB JR.

Christian psychologist Lawrence Crabb states that modern psychology has rightly concluded that one of man's most basic needs is personal worth.[20] Crabb states that there are two required inputs to make a person feel worthy. The two inputs are significance and security.[21]

To feel significant, each person must have a sense of purpose and a feeling of importance. One's life must be meaningful. One must have a definite impact on his world. To feel secure, a person must know he is loved unconditionally and eternally. If he does not feel eternally accepted, he will not feel secure.[22] Man longs for everlasting acceptance; temporary acceptance will not satisfy him.

Crabb argues that Adam and Eve had significance and security before the Fall, but once they alienated themselves from God through sin, they no longer felt significant and secure. [23] Since the Fall, significance and security have alluded man. Man has lost his sense of personal worth. Because of this, each person pretends to be someone he or she is not. Man also seeks significance and security in other people and in temporary pleasures, but inevitably true personal worth always evades man.

However, Crabb finds the solution to man's dilemma in the gospel. Once a person is saved, his needs for personal worth are met in Christ. Man is significant because God has given each person an eternal mission. The King of the universe has given every person a job to perform. He has called each individual to minister to others in His power and love. [24]

Man can also be secure, for God loved man enough to send His Son to die for him. God loves all people unconditionally. He loves all people just as they are, and He will never stop loving them. [25] Only in Jesus Christ can man find true personal worth.

CONCLUSION

Modern man seems more concerned with feelings than he does with reason. Because of this, psychological apologetics can be a very effective method of defending the faith in the present cultural climate.

If the God of the Bible does not exist, there is no hope for mankind. Man cannot experience true peace and joy knowing that he will someday cease to exist. If the God of the Bible does not exist, there can be no genuine meaning to life.

If God does not exist, objective moral values are nonexistent. Right is wrong and wrong is right. If there is no moral Lawgiver higher than man, there can be no moral law above man. Without life after death and a final judgment, it does not matter if one lives like Hitler or Mother Theresa. A million years from now, it will make no difference.

All men acknowledge the existence of evil (at least in their practice if not in their beliefs). But nothing less than the God of the Bible can guarantee the ultimate defeat of evil. Life is hopeless and without meaning if God does not exist.

Even the atheist philosopher Bertrand Russell acknowledged the absurdity of life without God. His rejection of God led him to refer to the universe as "purposeless" and "void of meaning."[26] Russell wrote:

> That man is the product of causes which had no prevision of the end they were achieving; that his origin, his growth, his hopes and fears, his loves and his beliefs, are but the outcome of accidental collocations of atoms; that no fire, no heroism, no intensity of thought and feeling, can preserve an individual life beyond the grave; that all the labors of the ages, all the devotion, all the inspiration, all the noonday brightness of human genius, are destined to extinction in the vast death of the solar system, and that the whole temple of man's achievement must inevitably be buried beneath the debris of a universe in ruins . . .[27]

Russell's world-without-God caused him to encourage his

followers to build their philosophy of life upon "the firm foundation of unyielding despair."[28]

Russell was right. If the God of the Bible does not exist, man is damned to a life of meaningless existence. To hide from this fact, a person can focus his attention on Pascalian diversions, or maybe a Kierkegaardian leap into the nonrational realm will be one's choice. But for those with the courage to deal with reality head on, a choice must be made between despair and the God of the Bible. As Pascal has said, the wise man will wager on God.

ENDNOTES

[1] Gordon H. Clark, *Thales to Dewey* (Jefferson: The Trinity Foundation, 1989), 3.

[2] Blaise Pascal, *Pensees* trans. A. J. Krailsheimer (New York: Penguin Books, 1966), 58.

[3] Ibid., 66.

[4] Ibid., 69.

[5] Ibid., 71.

[6] Ibid., 157.

[7] Ibid.

[8] Ibid., 160.

[9] Ibid., 156.

[10] Ibid., 165.

[11] Ibid., 149-155.

[12] Francis A. Schaeffer, *The Complete Works of Francis A. Schaeffer* (Westchester: Crossway Books, 1982), vol. 5, 178.

[13] Ibid., vol. 1, 10.

[14] Ibid., 232-233.

The God Who Sits Enthroned

[15] Ibid., 10.

[16] Ibid., 238.

[17] Ibid., 229.

[18] Gordon R. Lewis, *Testing Christianity's Truth Claims* (Lanham: University Press of America, 1990), 231-236.

[19] Ibid., 253.

[20] Lawrence J. Crabb Jr., *Effective Biblical Counseling* (Grand Rapids: Zondervan Publishing House, 1977), 61.

[21] Ibid.

[22] Ibid.

[23] Ibid.

[24] Ibid., 70.

[25] Ibid.

[26] Bertrand Russell, *Why I Am Not A Christian* (New York: Touchstone Books, 1957), 106.

[27] Ibid., 107.

[28] Ibid.

CHAPTER 2

Contemporary Man's Thirst For God

In the last chapter the absurdity of life without God was discussed. A similar aspect of psychological apologetics deals with contemporary man's thirst for God. Though many people currently deny or ignore the existence of the God of the Bible, their lives display a vacuum only He can fill.

ALL MEN THIRST FOR GOD

Christian philosophers Norman Geisler and Winfried Corduan argue that all "people sense a basic need for God."[1] The fact that Sigmund Freud attempted to explain this phenomena away shows that even he recognized this need for God in himself and others. (Of course, Freud denied that God exists.) Freud admitted that man feels powerless and insignificant in the face of the vast universe in which he finds himself.[2] According to Freud, man invents God through his imagination to calm his fears.

Friedrich Schleiermacher taught that all people have a feeling of absolute dependence, even though they do not all explain it in the same way. Both believers and nonbelievers alike recognize their absolute dependence on something that transcends their earthly experience.[3]

Martin Heidigger viewed man as a "being-unto-death."[4] Man finds himself thrown into the world. He has no say about his being here. He knows not why he is here, but there is one thing he does know. He knows he is destined for nothingness. Man had no control over his birth, and he can have no control over his death. He must die. Man finds himself thrust into this world en route to extinction. He is without a ground for his being. Man desperately needs a ground for his being.[5]

Paul Tillich recognized that man is limited and dependent. Man needs a ground for his being, something to anchor him in existence. Tillich spoke of this need as man's "ultimate concern."[6]

Jean-Paul Sartre, a French atheist, admitted his need for God. Sartre taught that man needs God to give his existence definition and meaning. But, since Sartre rejected God's existence, he felt that the entire project was absurd.[7] According to Sartre, man has a need for God, but there is no God who can meet this need.

Walter Kaufmann referred to man as the "God-intoxicated ape."[8] Friedrich Nietzsche considered his own atheistic views to be so unbearable that he wished he could be convinced he was wrong. He felt a strong thirst for God but rejected the possibility of God's real existence.[9]

Geisler and Corduan, after surveying the above list of non-Christian thinkers, arrived at the following conclusion:

> That people generally, if not universally, manifest a need for the Transcendent seems incontestable. The sense of contingency, the feeling of cosmic dependence, the need to believe in some sort of Transcendent is apparently present in all men. The residual but most essential question is this: Is there any basis in reality for this God-need which both believers and nonbelievers have confessed to having?[10]

The evidence indicates that all men sense a need for the God of the Bible. Even atheists and other non-Christians have expressed this need. Still, as Geisler and Corduan have noted, it must be shown that this need points to the actual existence of God.

THE FREUDIAN EXPLANATION

Though both atheists and Christians alike recognize the universal thirst for God, atheists deny that God actually exists. Instead, they speculate as to why so many people believe that He exists. An example of this kind of speculation is found in the thought of Sigmund Freud.

Freud was convinced that God did not exist. But if atheism is true, then why do so many people believe in God? Freud tried to answer this question. Freud suggested that primitive man felt extremely threatened by nature (due to storms, floods, earthquakes, diseases, and ultimately death).[11] Man had no control over nature. He was totally helpless in this regard. Primitive man was completely at the mercy of nature. There was nowhere man could turn for help. Freud theorized that primitive men therefore decided to personalize nature. In this way, man could attempt to plead with or appease nature.[12] Imagining nature to be a personal being enabled man to offer sacrifices to nature in hope that nature would be kind to him in return.

Freud's speculation did not stop there. He also promoted another theory of early human society. He assumed that originally mankind banded together in small groups. These clans consisted of a male, his several wives, and their offspring. Freud believed that, early in life, male children desired to have sex with their mothers. They therefore became extremely jealous of their father. Though they loved their father since he was their protector, they began to hate him due to their jealousy. Eventually, they banded together and murdered their father. After the murder, they ate the flesh of their father in a ritual meal. Soon, the male children were overcome with feelings of guilt. As a result, they deified the father image and began offering sacrifices to him as a god.[13]

Freud taught that God is nothing but a product of man's imagination. God did not create man. Instead, man created God. Man personalized nature due to his fear of nature. The guilt he felt for murdering his father also caused him to project the father image onto this personalized nature. In this way, reasoned Freud, the belief in the Father-God was originated by man's wishful thinking.

This highly speculative theory does not do justice to mankind's universal thirst for God. This theory appears to be "wishful thinking" on the part of Freud. Whatever the case, Freud's proposed explanation deserves a response.

A CHRISTIAN RESPONSE

Christian theologian R. C. Sproul is quick to point out that Freud's line of reasoning does not disprove God's existence. Instead, it presupposes His nonexistence. In other words, Freud was not trying to answer the question, "Does God exist?" Rather, he was attempting to answer the question, "Since God does not exist, why do so many people believe that He does?"[14]

Therefore, this speculation by Freud should not be viewed as a disproof of God's existence. It is simply a desperate attempt to explain away strong evidence for God's existence. It is an endeavor which focuses on answering the question, "If atheism is true, why are there so few atheists?" Freud answers the question by accusing all who disagree with him of being deluded.

Sproul points out that Freud's speculation explains how men use their imaginations to invent idols (false gods) but not the God of the Bible. For the God of the Bible is far too demanding. No one would wish for the existence of a Being that requires the submission and obedience demanded by the Christian God. The gods of other religions are attractive candidates for projection, but the Holy God of the Scriptures is the type of Being from whom men run. No one would invent Him through wishful thinking.[15]

Christian philosopher J. P. Moreland states that "atheism is a result of a desire to kill the father figure (in Freudian language) because one wishes to be autonomous."[16] Man's two greatest drives are his thirst for God and his desire to be autonomous. Man has a void that can only be filled by God. Still, man wants to be his own king. The Christian chooses God over autonomy. The atheist, on the other hand, chooses autonomy.

Moreland adds that even if Freud was right, his argument would still be guilty of what philosophers call the genetic fallacy.[17] The genetic fallacy claims that a belief can be shown to be false just by showing its origin is unreasonable. But this is not the case. Even if mankind, due to fear and guilt, originated the idea of God, this does not prove that God does not exist. God might still exist even if people arrived at this conclusion through faulty reasoning.

Christian philosophers Norman Geisler and Winfried Corduan argue that what people really need actually exists.[18] Humans need food and water. Food and water exist. Even if a person dies of thirst or hunger, the fact is that food and water do exist. It is just that the person did not find them. Geisler and Corduan argue that all men really need God. The thirst for God is universal. As shown above, even many atheists admit to this fact. God is not something people merely desire. He is something people need. And since whatever man needs exists, then God exists.[19] This would be true even if a person does not find God (as some people do not find food or water). This argument is not meant to be an air-tight proof, but it does seem to have a high degree of probability (everything else man needs does in fact exist).

CONCLUSION

If all men have a void that only God can fill, then one would expect the Bible to address this issue, and this, of course, is the case. Jesus said, "Man shall not live on bread alone, but on every word that proceeds out of the mouth of God" (Matthew 4:4). Man is more than a physical being. He is also a spiritual being. Not only does man need physical nourishment, he also needs spiritual nourishment from the true God. Jesus proclaimed, "I am the bread of life; he who comes to me shall not hunger, and he who believes in me shall never thirst" (John 6:35). Only Jesus can quench our thirst for God.

Unfortunately, most people attempt to quench this thirst with unworthy substitutes which can never meet their most ultimate needs. The Word of God declares, "For My people have committed two evils: they have forsaken Me, the fountain of living waters, to hew for themselves cisterns, broken cisterns, that can hold no water" (Jeremiah 2:13). Rather than turn to Christ, most people look elsewhere to find fulfillment in life. For some, their "broken cistern" is a false religion. For others, it is material wealth. Many people try sexual immorality, drugs, or alcohol. But there is no worthy substitute for the true living water. Only Jesus can meet man's deepest needs.

As mentioned earlier, the two strongest drives in man are his thirst for God and his desire for autonomy (he wants to be his own king). Jesus was aware of this. He addressed this issue during His conversation with Nicodemus. Jesus stated:

> And this is the judgment, that the light is come
> into the world, and men loved the darkness rather
> than the light; for their deeds were evil. For every-
> one who does evil hates the light, and does not
> come to the light, lest his deeds should be
> exposed. But he who practices the truth comes to
> the light, that his deeds may be manifested as hav-
> ing been wrought in God (John 3:19-21).

Those who place their need for God above their desire to
be in complete control of their lives will find Christ. On the
other hand, those who continually refuse to surrender their
autonomy to God will never come to Jesus. Because the
thirst for God resides within the hearts of all men, we must
offer them living water. Man will never find ultimate fulfillment in life without trusting in the Lord Jesus Christ. Only
then will his thirst for God be quenched. As Augustine has
prayed, ". . . you made us for yourself and our hearts find no
peace until they rest in you."[20]

ENDNOTES

[1] Norman Geisler and Winfried Corduan, *Philosophy of Religion* (Grand
Rapids: Baker Book House, 1988), 69.

[2] Ibid., 69-70.

[3] Ibid., 70.

[4] Ibid.

[5] Ibid., 70-71.

[6] Ibid., 71·

[7] Ibid., 71-72.

[8] Ibid., 72.

[9] Friedrich Nietzsche, *The Portable Nietzsche*, ed. Walter Kaufmann (New York: Penguin Books, 1982), 441.

[10] Geisler and Corduan, 72-73.

[11] Sigmund Freud, *The Future of an Illusion*, trans. W. D. Robson-Scott (New York: Doubleday, 1964), 20.

[12] R. C. Sproul, *If There's a God, Why are There Atheists?* (Wheaton: Tyndale House Publishers, 1978), 42-44.

[13] Ninian Smart, *The Religious Experience of Mankind* (New York: Charles Scribner's Sons, 1976), 40.

[14] Sproul, 49.

[15] Ibid., 12, 58, 101.

[16] J. P. Moreland, *Scaling the Secular City* (Grand Rapids: Baker Book House, 1987), 229.

[17] Ibid.

[18] Geisler and Corduan, 74.

[19] Ibid., 74-75.

[20] Saint Augustine, *Confessions*, trans. R. S. Pine-Coffin (London: Penguin Books, 1961), 21.

CHAPTER 3

Man's Greatness and Wretchedness

Psychological apologetics has been used to remind man that though he is great and noble, he is also wretched and cruel. Defenders of the faith must show that Christianity alone offers an adequate explanation for this dilemma of man. Man was created in God's image (man's greatness) but he has fallen (man's wretchedness).

BLAISE PASCAL

Pascal taught that neither man's greatness nor his wretchedness should be overlooked. He stated, "It is dangerous to explain too clearly to man how like he is to the animals without pointing out his greatness." [1] Pascal added, "It is also dangerous to make too much of his greatness without his vileness." [2] "It is still more dangerous to leave him in ignorance of both, but it is most valuable to represent both to him."[3]

Pascal declared that "Man's greatness comes from knowing he is wretched: a tree does not know it is wretched."[4] He reasons that, "All these examples of wretchedness prove his greatness. It is the wretchedness of a great lord, the wretchedness of a dispossessed king."[5] Pascal concludes that man "must have fallen from some better state which was once his own. Who indeed would think himself unhappy not to be a king except one who had been dispossessed?"[6]

Pascal describes the current state of man when he says that men "retain some feeble instinct from the happiness of their first nature . . ." and that they are "plunged into the wretchedness of their blindness and concupiscence, which has become their second nature."[7] Going further, Pascal states:

> Man is only a reed, the weakest in nature, but he is a thinking reed. There is no need for the whole universe to take up arms to crush him: a vapor, a drop of water is enough to kill him. But even if the universe were to crush him, man would still be nobler than his slayer, because he knows that he is dying and the advantage the universe has over him. The universe knows none of this. Thus all our dignity consists in thought.[8]

Pascal challenges his readers with the following words:

> Man's greatness and wretchedness are so evident that the true religion must necessarily teach us that

there is in man some great principle of greatness and some great principle of wretchedness. It must also account for such amazing contradictions . . . Let us examine all the religions of the world on that point and let us see whether any but the Christian religion meets it.[9]

Pascal detected in man a greatness not found in the animal kingdom. But he also found in man a wretchedness that he shared with animals. Pascal believed that the true religion, whatever it is, must explain this dilemma of man. He concluded that Christianity alone adequately treats this issue.

FRANCIS SCHAEFFER

Francis Schaeffer states that "Anyone with sensitivity and concern for the world can see that man is in a great dilemma. Man is able both to rise to great heights and to sink to great depths of cruelty and tragedy."[10] Schaeffer speaks of the *nobility of man* as well the *cruelty of man*. Schaeffer declares, "So man stands with all his wonder and nobility, and yet also with his horrible cruelty that runs throughout the warp and woof of man's history."[11]

Schaeffer, in his attempt to explain the fact of man's nobility and cruelty, suggests that the only answer to the dilemma is the Christian answer. Man was created perfect and in God's image. But man has fallen into sin. Schaeffer states:

In the area of morals, we have nothing of these answers except on the basis of a true, space-time, historic Fall. There was a time before the Fall, and then man turned from his proper integration point by choice; and in so doing, there was a moral discontinuity—man became abnormal.[12]

In the tradition of Pascal, Schaeffer sees Christianity as the only solution to the dilemma of man. Without the doctrines of creation and the Fall, there would be no explanation for the greatness and wretchedness of man.

WEAKNESSES OF THE EVOLUTIONARY EXPLANATION

Many atheists have proposed the evolution hypothesis as another possible explanation for man's nobility and cruelty. Still, there are two weaknesses with the evolutionary hypothesis that cause it to fall short of offering an adequate explanation of man's dilemma. First, evolution implies that man is moving towards greatness, not away from it. Man, according to this view, is getting better. But the wars of the twentieth century have been the bloodiest of all time. There is much talk of peace, but men continue to war with one other. If anything, man is getting worse.

Second, man's greatness does not appear to be merely the next stage in animal development. Rather, it seems to be distinctly that which separates men from the animals. There seems to be a gap at this point that cannot be traversed. As one examines the animal kingdom, there is an advancement from one species to another that cannot be denied (although the evolutionary doctrine of common ancestry can be called into question). However, the advancement between man and animal is too great. The greatness of man is not a point of continuity with the animal kingdom. It is a point of discontinuity. It argues against evolution, not for it.

CONCLUSION

Pascal and Schaeffer were both right to point out the greatness and wretchedness of man. Man's greatness can be seen in many ways. His selfless acts of heroism, charitable giving, and caring for the less fortunate all attest to the greatness of man. Still, the builder of hospitals is also the builder of torture chambers. The history of mankind is filled with more than just acts of heroism. It records horrible murders. For every act of charity, there may be several acts of thievery.

Pascal and Schaeffer are also correct in declaring Christianity to be the only religion that deals adequately with man's greatness and his wretchedness. All other world religions downplay the wretchedness of man by teaching that man is good enough to save himself. There is an overemphasis on man's greatness and an underemphasis on man's wretchedness. Only Christianity offers the proper balance.

The argument for Christianity which begins with the greatness and wretchedness of man can be very effective. However, its effectiveness will depend upon how well the apologist uncovers the deficiencies of all other proposed solutions offered by non-Christian belief systems. The Christian must show that man's greatness can only be explained if man was created perfect and in God's image.

The believer must also show that only the Fall adequately explains man's wretchedness.

ENDNOTES

[1] Pascal, *Pensees*, 60.

[2] Ibid.

[3] Ibid.

[4] Ibid., 59.

[5] Ibid.

[6] Ibid.

[7] Ibid., 77.

[8] Ibid., 95.

[9] Ibid., 76.

[10] Schaeffer, *Complete Works*, vol. 1, 109.

[11] Ibid., 293.

[12] Ibid., 304.

PART TWO

Philosophical Apologetics

CHAPTER 4

The Failure of Atheism

Philosophical Apologetics deals with the rational defense of the Christian Faith. Philosophy means the love of wisdom.[1] One of the functions of philosophy is the attempt to describe the true nature of reality.[2] Philosophy of religion (a branch of philosophy) and apologetics (a branch of theology) overlap in certain areas.[3] Arguments for God's existence, the philosophical problem of evil, the possibility of miracles, and the nature of morality are common to both philosophy of religion and apologetics. These topics will be examined in this section.

ATHEISM AND AGNOSTICISM

Atheism is the belief that it can be proven that God does not exist.[4] Agnosticism, on the other hand, is the belief that man cannot know whether or not God exists.[5] It is possible to hold weaker forms of either view.[6] However, this chapter is only concerned with refuting the more dogmatic forms of atheism and agnosticism. Only the stronger forms, if proven, would defeat theism. (The weaker forms leave open the possibility of theism.) However, both atheism and agnosticism, in their strongest forms, are self-refuting.

In order for one to disprove God's existence (atheism), he would be all-knowing,[7] and he would have the ability to see and know all things in the physical and spiritual realms. In short, one would have to be God to disprove God's existence. Of course, this is absurd.

Agnosticism is also self-defeating. One must know something about God to know that nothing can be known about God.[8] Obviously, this statement refutes itself. Therefore, agnosticism, like atheism, is a self-refuting view.

Many agnostics say that since man is finite (limited), he can never attain knowledge of an infinite (unlimited) Being. It is true that the finite cannot find the infinite on its own. However, this ignores the possibility that the infinite Being may choose to reveal Himself to finite beings. This is exactly what Christianity claims. The Bible teaches that God reveals Himself through both nature (Romans 1:18-22; Psalms 19:1) and the scriptures (2 Timothy 3:16-17; 2 Peter 1:20-21).

DID MAN INVENT GOD?

Throughout history thinkers proclaimed their belief that God was a product of man's imagination. Ludwig Feuerbach (1804-1872) taught that man, due to his fear of death, wishes God into existence. Man recognizes his limitations and fears. God is projected to calm these fears. In short, God is what man wishes to be.[9]

Sigmund Freud (1856-1939) saw two separate causes for man's belief in God. First, Freud believed that each boy desires to have sexual relations with his mother. Because of this, he becomes jealous of his father and develops a hatred for him. Second, since man could not fully understand the forces of nature, he began to fear nature. Freud concluded that due to these two factors (man's guilt for hating his father and man's fear of nature), mankind deified nature and personalized it into a Father God.[10]

It should be understood that the speculations of Feuerbach and Freud were never meant to be used as arguments against God's existence. Instead, these two thinkers believed that God's existence had already been proven false by the advances of modern science. Their views were promoted not to disprove God's existence. Rather, they were promoted as a desperate attempt to explain why nearly all of mankind believes in a non-existent God. Therefore, the ideas of Feuerbach and Freud should not be considered evidence against God's existence. Instead, their theories were merely attempts to explain away some of the evidence against their views.[11]

Freud's own theories can be used against him. For it seems more likely that *atheism* is caused by the desire to kill the father image, rather than theism being caused by man's guilt for wanting to kill his father.[12] In man's attempt to be autonomous, he wishes God out of existence.

Whatever the case, the speculations of Feuerbach and

Freud seem to be wishful thinking by atheists. If men were to invent a God, it is doubtful that it would be the demanding God of the Bible.[13] Man would create a more permissive god, much like the gods of the pagan religions. In short, the theories of Feuerbach and Freud offer a more adequate explanation for atheism and idolatry than they do for Christianity.[14]

A. J. AYER AND LOGICAL POSITIVISM

In the first half of this century, A. J. Ayer and his colleagues popularized their view of logical positivism. Logical positivism was based upon the verification principle. This principle stated that for a statement to be meaningful, it has to be either true by definition or verifiable by one or more of the five senses.[15] This meant that all discussion about God should be considered meaningless.[16]

If true, this view would be very damaging for theism. Though it would not prove God's nonexistence, it would make all talk about God meaningless.[17] If one cannot meaningfully talk about God, one cannot speculate about his possible existence.

However, the problem with the verification principle is that it is itself not true by definition or verifiable by one or more of the five senses.[18] In other words, the verification principle is self-refuting. If the verification principle is true, then it is itself meaningless, for it fails its own test.[19]

If atheism is to deliver a fatal blow to theism, it will have to look elsewhere. Logical positivism has failed to render discussion about God meaningless.

IS RELIGIOUS LANGUAGE EQUIVOCAL?

Some have maintained that all talk about God is equivocal.[20] In other words, they believe that terms used to describe God have totally different meanings than when they are used in connection with finite beings such as man. If this is true, then man cannot know anything about God. If someone says God is holy, he has uttered a meaningless statement. For man knows what holiness means only when it refers to a man. Man has no idea of what holiness means when applied to God. What holiness means in reference to an infinite being (God) cannot be known by finite beings. If the theist is justified in his or her claims to know something about God, then this objection must be answered.

Some theists have argued that terms used to describe God are univocal.[21] This means that they have totally the same meaning when used to describe both God and man. The problem with this view is that it is hard to believe that God is holy in the same way that man can be holy. For God is infinitely holy, whereas man is only finitely holy. Can holiness have the exact meaning for both man and God? Obviously not.

Other atheists contend that religious language is analogical.[22] They hold that terms used of God and man are not equivocal (totally different meanings) or univocal (totally the same meanings). Instead, terms used of God and man are only analogical (similar meanings). However, this view is also problematic. For if God-talk is analogical, then theologians are still using meaningless terms about God. For terms like "holiness" still lack the same meaning they hold when used of men. We can only know what holiness means when it is applied to man. It appears that there must be some univocal element to God-talk if it is to be meaningful.[23]

The answer to this dilemma comes from Thomas Aquinas. He reasoned that words have the same meaning (univocal) when applied to either God or man. However, Aquinas taught that they can only be applied in a similar (analogical) way.[24] Therefore, holiness means the same thing for both man and God. Still, it must be applied finitely to man and infinitely to God. Therefore, God-talk is not equivocal. Theists can meaningfully talk about God.

JEAN-PAUL SARTRE AND EXISTENTIALISM

Jean-Paul Sartre was a famous French philosopher and existentialist. He argued that if the theist persists in his assertion that everything needs a cause, then even God needs a cause. Therefore, the theist, according to Sartre, must argue that God caused His own existence. But, this would make God a self-caused being, which is impossible.[25] For a being to cause its own existence, it must exist before it existed in order to bring itself into existence. However, it is absurd to say that a being existed before it existed. Therefore, reasoned Sartre, since God is a self-caused being, He cannot exist.

However, no informed theist believes that everything (including God) needs a cause. Only dependent beings (beings that have a beginning) need a cause. Since God is an independent and eternal being, He does not need a cause.[26] God is not a self-caused being. He is an uncaused being. His existence needs no cause for He always existed.

Sartre also contended that since man is free, God cannot exist. In his view, if man is free (and Sartre believed so), then there could be no sovereign God. If a sovereign God exists, then men are robots.[27]

There have been two ways that theists respond to this argument. One can take a hyper-Calvinistic position and deny human free will.[28] Or, one can simply maintain that God sovereignly chose to make man free.[29] Still, man is not absolutely free. He is free to disobey God and reject Christ, but he is not free to escape the God-ordained consequences of his actions. In short, neither of Sartre's objections presents insurmountable problems for theism.

BERTRAND RUSSELL

The great British philosopher and mathematician Bertrand Russell reasoned that if everything needs a cause, then so does God. But if God doesn't need a cause, then neither does the universe.[30] As mentioned above, the theist responds to this by pointing out that not everything needs a cause. Only that which has a beginning needs a cause. Since God does not have a beginning, He needs no cause.[31]

Secondly, there is both scientific and philosophical evidence that the universe had a beginning. Scientific evidence consists in the second law of thermodynamics (energy deterioration) and the big bang model. The second law of thermodynamics shows that the amount of usable energy in the universe is running down. Therefore, the universe will eventually cease to exist when all its energy is used up. But if the universe will have an end, it had to have a beginning. This means that the universe began with all its energy in a usable state. Hence, the universe had a beginning.[32]

The big bang model reveals that the universe is expanding at an equal rate in all directions. This is much like the effects of an explosion which blows debris in all directions. If one goes back in time, the universe would become more and more dense until the entire universe would be compressed into an infinitely small point. This would mark the beginning of the universe.[33]

The scientific evidence for the beginning of the universe does not stand alone. Philosophical evidence can be found as well. For if the universe is eternal, there would be an infinite amount of actual events in the past. But then it would be impossible to reach the present moment. For no matter how many events one traverses, there will always be an infinite amount of events left. Hence, the present moment could never be reached. But the present moment has been reached. This proves that there is only a finite number of events in the past. Therefore, the universe had a first event. In other words, the universe had a beginning.[34]

Bertrand Russell's objection therefore loses its force. The universe cannot be eternal. It must have a cause. Eventually one must arrive at a first cause, a being that needs no cause. This uncaused being is what the theist calls God.

ALBERT CAMUS

The French existentialist Albert Camus authored the novel entitled *The Plague*. In this work, Camus argued that if God allowed the plague to occur, then to fight the plague is to fight God. Therefore, to be religious, one must be anti-humanitarian. Only the atheist can be a humanitarian and remain consistent with his beliefs.[35]

Camus' argument has been adequately answered. Even though God permits the plague (symbolic for evil and human suffering) for the purpose of a greater good, He is nonetheless working to defeat the plague.[36] In fact, the greater good coming from God permitting the plague may include the godly man joining God to battle the plague.[37] Just because God allows something to occur does not make it in itself good. For God could and does allow evil to occur for the purpose of a good that He will bring from the evil.

Therefore, a person can be religious and also be humanitarian without going against his or her beliefs. On the other hand, what is to prevent the atheist from doing whatever he pleases? It seems that the Christian humanitarian is more consistent with his or her beliefs than the atheist is. For in atheism there is no final judgment and moral values are mere human inventions. Atheists are not being consistent with their world view whenever they condemn an action as wrong.

ANTONY FLEW

British philosopher Antony Flew claims that since there is no way to falsify God's existence, to assert that He does exist is an incoherent statement.[38] Flew is famous for his parable of the invisible gardener.[39] In this parable, a believer and a non-believer come upon a garden in the midst of the wilderness. The believer assumes that there exists a gardener who cares for the garden. The non-believer, however, disagrees. He concludes that there is no gardener. They were not able to detect the existence of the gardener though they ran several tests. They did not see or hear him enter the garden. Even bloodhounds could not smell him. Rather than surrender his faith in the gardener, the believer reasons that the gardener must be invisible and unable to be detected by the five senses. The non-believer responds by stating that there is no difference between this invisible gardener and no gardener at all. In other words, if there is no way to falsify a view, then the view is worthless.[40]

Flew declares that just as there is no way to falsify the existence of the invisible gardener, so too the existence of the Christian God cannot be falsified. In short, to claim that God exists is to make a meaningless statement. There is no way to prove it false; nothing is allowed to count against it.

In response to Flew's objection, several things can be noted. First, the believer views the universe as dependent and in need of a cause. If there were no independent God, there would also be no dependent universe. If the universe could be shown to exist independent of any cause, then this would go a long way to falsifying the God hypothesis. However, scientific and philosophical arguments for an eternal and independent universe have not been successful. Recent thought seems to lead in the other direction.[41]

Second, the God of the Bible is not a silent God who is unable to be detected. The Judeo-Christian scriptures are filled with prophecies that were fulfilled hundreds of years after they were recorded.[42] If these prophecies had failed, then the God of the Bible would be falsified.

Third, Christianity claims that the God of the Bible has become a man (John 1:1,14). The invisible gardener has taken visible form. Jesus claimed to be God incarnate. Jesus gave persuasive evidence for this claim by performing numerous miracles in the presence of eyewitnesses. His greatest miracle was when He rose from the dead and appeared to many eyewitnesses. If the first century Jewish religious leaders had produced the rotting corpse of Christ, they would have falsified Christ's claims and crushed Christianity in its embryonic form. Despite the fact that the Jewish religious leaders had the desire to do so, they did not produce the body.

What needs to be noted here is that the belief in the existence of the God of the Bible is open to testing and falsification. Instead of claiming that God is an incoherent concept incapable of being falsified, Flew would do better to examine the evidence for the Christian God and then attempt to prove as false the claim that He exists.

ARGUMENTS FROM CONTRADICTORY ATTRIBUTES

One attempt to refute the existence of God is to claim that the God of the Bible has certain characteristics that are contradictory.[43] If this can be proven, the Christian God cannot exist. This atheistic endeavor can take its form in several different arguments. Two examples will suffice.

Atheists often argue that if God is all-powerful, then He can do anything. This would include the ability to create a rock so large that even He cannot lift it. But if God cannot lift this rock, He is not all-powerful. Therefore, concludes the atheist, no all-powerful God can exist.[44]

Though the theist agrees that God is all-powerful, he recognizes that there are some things that even an all-powerful being cannot do. Since an all-powerful being will always be able to accomplish whatever He sets out to do, it is impossible for an all-powerful being to fail. The above atheistic argument is arguing that since God is all-powerful He can do anything, even fail. This is like saying that since God is all-powerful He can be not all-powerful. Obviously, this is absurd. An all-powerful being cannot fail. Therefore, God can create a rock of tremendous size, but, since He is all-powerful, He will always be able to lift it.[45]

There are several things that an all-powerful being cannot do: He cannot lie, sin, or change His mind (Numbers 23:19; James 1:13; 1 Samuel 15:29). Anything that indicates failure cannot be attributed to God.[46]

It should also be noted that God cannot do whatever is impossible by definition. For instance, God cannot create square circles.[47] He cannot create a human that is non-human. He cannot make something both exist and not exist at the same time.

In short, when one says that God is all-powerful, one means that God is able to accomplish all that He desires to do. It means that God can do everything that is possible.[48] But even an all-powerful being cannot do what is impossible by definition. God can do many things that are humanly impossible. However, there are some things that even an all-powerful being cannot do.

Therefore, since God is all-powerful, He will always be

able to master His creation. He will always be able to lift any rock that He creates. And, since all that exists (besides Himself) is His creation, there is no rock, nor will there ever be a rock, that He cannot lift.

A second example of an argument against God from supposed contradictory attributes is as follows. If something is good simply because God wills it, then good is merely an arbitrary concept. But, if God wills it because it is good, then good is a standard above God. Therefore, either good is arbitrary or good is above God.[49]

If the theist concedes either of these two propositions, the concept of God will be damaged. For if good is arbitrary, then calling God good says nothing more than He does what He wills to do. He doesn't do what is right. He simply acts arbitrarily. Whatever He does automatically is considered right for the mere reason that it is an act of God.

If the theist takes the other alternative of the dilemma, the situation is no better. For if God decides to do something because it is good, it appears that there is a standard of right and wrong above God. But then God would not be the ultimate being. A necessary element of the traditional Christian concept of God is that He is the ultimate being. There is no being greater than God (not even goodness). However, God cannot be the ultimate being if there is a standard of right and wrong to which He must submit. The standard itself would be the ultimate being since it would be above God.

Those who use this objection against theism fail to acknowledge that God wills something because it is consistent with His own good nature. Therefore, the standard is not above God; God is the standard.[50] Thus, good is not arbitrary, for it is based upon God's good nature.[51]

THE PROBLEM OF EVIL

Many atheists believe that the existence of evil is proof that an all-good and all-powerful God does not exist.[52] The significance of this argument is such that an entire chapter of this work be dedicated to its refutation. Therefore, discussion of this atheistic objection will be dealt with in a later chapter of this book.

THE REAL PROBLEM WITH ATHEISTS

According to the Bible, the real problem with atheists is not an intellectual one. Rather it is a moral problem. It is not that there is insufficient evidence for God's existence. Instead, the atheist chooses not to submit to the Creator. The Bible declares that those who act upon the truth will come to the light of Christ (John 3:16-21). On the other hand, those who suppress the truth of God's existence are without excuse. For the invisible God has revealed His existence and power through His visible creation (Romans 1:18-23).

It appears that there are two opposing drives in each person. One is a thirst for God (John 6:35). The other is the drive for human autonomy (Romans 3:10-12). If a persons seeks God with all his heart, he will find Him (Jeremiah 29:13). But if he chooses to continually reject the Creator, there is no amount of evidence that will change his mind. All that the Christian apologist can do is provide evidence for the existence of the God of the Bible and to refute arguments for atheism. Once a strong case for Christian Theism is made, the atheist must still choose to accept or reject the evidence. The inward persuasion of the Holy Spirit on the heart of the nonbeliever is necessary, but, in the end, the atheist must choose to follow that persuasion. The ultimate problem is not one of the intellect; it is a moral problem of the will. When all is said and done, one must choose God.

ENDNOTES

[1] Norman Geisler and Paul Feinberg, *Introduction to Philosophy* (Grand Rapids: Baker Book House, 1980),13.

[2] Ibid., 17.

[3] Ronald H. Nash, *Faith and Reason* (Grand Rapids: Zondervan Publishing House, 1988), 13-14.

[4] Geisler and Feinberg, 430.

[5] Ibid., 429.

[6] Ibid., 296.

[7] Norman Geisler, *Christian Apologetics* (Grand Rapids: Baker Book House, 1976), 233.

[8] Geisler and Feinberg, 298-299.

[9] William S. Sahakian, *History of Philosophy* (New York: Harper Collins Publishers, 1968), 202.

[10] Sigmund Freud, *The Future of an Illusion*, 20-27.

[11] Sproul, 49-50.

[12] Moreland, *Scaling the Secular City*, 229.

[13] Sproul, 58, 145-146.

[14] Ibid.

[15] Geisler and Feinberg, 50.

[16] Ibid.

[17] Ibid.

[18] Ibid.

[19] Ibid.

[20] Geisler and Corduan, 252-271.

[21] Ibid., 252.

[22] Ibid., 253.

[23] Ibid., 255.

[24] Ibid., 263-264.

[25] Geisler and Feinberg, 293.

[26] Ibid.

[27] Ibid., 295.

[28] Ibid.

[29] Ibid.

[30] Bertrand Russell, 6-7.

[31] Geisler and Feinberg, 293.

[32] Roy E. Peacock, *A Brief History of Eternity* (Wheaton: Crossway Books, 1990), 67-69.

[33] Hugh Ross, *The Creator and the Cosmos* (Colorado Springs: NavPress, 1993), 19-27.

[34] William Lane Craig, *Apologetics, An Introduction* (Chicago: Moody Press, 1984), 81.

[35] Geisler and Corduan, 365.

[36] Ibid., 365-366.

[37] Ibid.

[38] John Hick, ed. *The Existence of God* (New York: The Macmillian Company, 1964), 224-226.

[39] Ibid.

[40] Ibid.

[41] Craig, 73-95.

[42] Henry M. Morris, *Many Infallible Proofs* (El Cajon: Master Books, 1974), 181-199.

[43] Geisler and Feinberg, 294.

[44] Ibid., 294-295.

[45] Ibid., 273-274.

[46] Geisler, *Apologetics*, 229.

[47] Ibid.

[48] Ibid.

[49] Geisler and Feinberg, 226.

[50] Ibid.

[51] Ibid.

[52] Geisler and Corduan, 295-385.

CHAPTER 5

The Failure of Other Non-Theistic World Views

Theism is the view of reality which holds to the existence of a personal God who is separate (transcendent) from the universe though involved (immanent) with it.[1] Christianity, Judaism, and Islam are the three main theistic religions.[2]

It has been shown that atheism, the world view that there is no God, has failed to prove its case. This means that theism may be true. It is therefore possible that God exists. However, before looking into arguments for the existence of the theistic God, discussion of other non-theistic world views is necessary to show that they have also failed to prove their cases.

The non-theistic world views (other than atheism) include

pantheism, panentheism, deism, finite godism, and polytheism. If these world views fail as atheism has failed, then the case for theism will become more probable since it is the only remaining major world view. Of course, the case for theism will reach a high degree of probability only if strong arguments can be advanced in its favor.

PANTHEISM

Pantheism is the world view that teaches that God is the universe.[3] Pantheism is based upon monism, the belief that all reality is one being.[4] Hinduism and some adherents of Buddhism are pantheistic in their thought.[5] The New Age Movement (the invasion of Western Society with Hindu thought) is also pantheistic.[6]

Pantheism teaches that God is not a personal being. Instead, God is an impersonal force.[7] Since pantheists believe that all reality is one being and that God is this one reality, they believe that each individual is God.[8] In fact, individual existence is merely an illusion since all reality is one being.[9]

There are several problems for pantheism which cause it to fail as a world view. First, many beings exist, not just one.[10] As Christian philosopher Norman Geisler has pointed out, it is actually undeniable that I exist.[11] For if I attempt to deny my existence, I must first exist to make the denial.[12] For nothing can deny nothing. Only an existent being can deny its own existence. Therefore, I exist. However, if I try to convince others that I alone exist, I must first affirm their own individual and separate existence by communicating with them.[13] In other words, to argue for pantheism is to admit that pantheism is false. To argue with others is to affirm the existence of others, and if more than one being exists, then pantheism cannot be true.

A second problem with pantheism is that there is strong evidence that the universe had a beginning. Both the big bang model and the second law of thermodynamics reveal this.[14] Also, if the universe is eternal, the present moment could never have arrived. But since the present moment has arrived, only a finite number of events could have occurred in the past.[15] Therefore, there was a first event. The universe had a beginning. Since from nothing, nothing comes, everything that had a beginning needs a cause. Hence, the universe needs a cause.[16] But, for pantheism to be true, the universe would have to be eternal and uncaused.

Third, pantheism claims that reality is ultimately impersonal. This is the same as saying that reality is non-intelligent and non-moral.[17] But for someone to deny the reality of intelligence, he must first assume he has the intelligence to make the denial.[18] Even pantheists pass moral judgments on others. In fact, many pantheists have been known to protest violence and the production of nuclear weapons.[19] They have fought for stricter anti-pollution legislation and campaigned for animal rights.[20] It is hard to find a pantheist who is not vocal about his or her moral beliefs. Pantheists must explain where intelligence and morality come from. Could intelligence and morality have been caused by a non-intelligent and non-moral being? It appears more probable that the Ultimate Cause of intelligence and morality must Himself be an intelligent and moral Being.[21]

Fourth, why should anyone accept the pantheistic claim that the world is an illusion? Does not common sense and experience favor the reality of the physical world? Why should anyone embrace pantheism without any evidence when common sense and experience teach otherwise?[22]

For these four reasons it appears that pantheism as a world view has failed. If an alternative to theism is to be found, one must look elsewhere.

PANENTHEISM

Panentheism has been described as the belief that the universe is God's body.[23] In this world view, God is conceived of as having two poles to His existence. In His potential pole, He is infinite, unchanging, and eternal. In His actual pole, He is finite, changing, and temporal.[24] Unlike pantheism, panentheism views God as personal.[25]

However, panentheism fails for several reasons. First, God cannot be both infinite and finite. This would be the same as saying that God is both unlimited and limited,[26] and this is an obvious contradiction. The Christian concept of God is one of an infinite God in His basic nature.[27] Panentheism, on the other hand, holds the contradictory concept of a God who is both infinite and finite in His basic nature.

Second, panentheism is again contradictory when it declares God to be both eternal (without a beginning) and temporal (with a beginning).[28] One cannot have it both ways. Either God is eternal or God is temporal. In the Christian doctrine of the incarnation, the eternal God added a temporal nature to his eternal nature.[29] This involves no contradiction, but, in the case of panentheism, a contradiction is evident. If the eternal pole of God caused the temporal pole of God to come into existence, then it would make more sense for the panentheist to refer to the temporal pole not as God, but as God's creation. But then the panentheist would cease to be a panentheist. In fact, he would then be a theist.[30]

Third, panentheism teaches that God actualizes His own potentialities. However, this is impossible. No potentiality can actualize itself. For instance, empty cups cannot fill themselves. For a potentiality to become actual, something actual must actualize it. As a result, the panentheistic god, if it existed, would need the theistic God to actualize its potential to exist.[31] Therefore, panentheism also fails as a world view.

DEISM

Deism is the world view that promotes the belief in a God who created the universe but no longer has any dealings with it.[32] The deist believes that God allows the world to operate on its own in accordance with natural laws that He has set in motion.[33] God does not perform miracles or interrupt the natural course of events.[34]

Thomas Jefferson, Benjamin Franklin, and Thomas Paine were deists of the eighteenth century.[35] Though deism is not as popular as it once was, similar views are held today by many Unitarians and religious humanists.[36]

Several objections to deism deserve mention. First, deists deny a miracle-working God. Yet, they admit one of God's greatest supernatural works when they affirm His work of creation. If God could create the entire universe out of nothing, then could He not perform lesser miracles?[37]

Second, if God cared enough to create the universe, then why doesn't He care enough to be involved with it?[38] And, third, the deistic view of natural laws is outdated. Natural laws are now considered by scientists to be descriptive of the general way nature acts. No longer are natural laws thought to prescribe what can and cannot happen in nature.[39] Natural laws cannot automatically rule out miracles, just as the occurrence of usual events does not disprove the possibility of unusual events occurring.[40]

In the seventeenth and eighteenth centuries, deism was a strong movement.[41] Much of its popularity was due to the belief that the science of that day had proven miracles to be impossible.[42] However, now that this misconception has been overturned, deism is no longer the attractive world view that it once was.

FINITE GODISM

Finite Godism is a world view that accepts the existence of a god. However, it believes He is limited.[43] Adherents differ as to how God is limited. Some believe He is limited in His power.[44] Others consider Him limited in His knowledge or His goodness.[45]

Devotees of Finite Godism usually promote their world view as the answer to the problem of evil.[46] They reason that an all-good and all-powerful God would not allow evil and innocent humans to suffer in the world.[47] Rabbi Harold Kushner, author of *When Bad Things Happen to Good People*, holds this view. He believes that evil proves God is not perfect and that He is limited in power.[48] For if God could prevent it, reasons Kushner, God would not allow the innocent to suffer.[49] Kushner asks others to forgive God for His failures.[50]

Several responses have been given to overthrow belief in the existence of a finite God. First, all finite existence needs a cause for its continuing existence.[51] Finite beings are, by definition, limited beings. And limited beings, precisely because of their limitations, must depend on other beings to keep them in existence. In fact, if everything that exists is limited and dependent, then nothing would now exist. For there must exist an infinite Being that is the cause of the continuing existence of all finite and dependent beings. In other words, a finite God would depend on an infinite God for its existence. However, a finite God would not be God after all. Only the infinite Being is God.[52]

Second, a finite God doesn't deserve worship.[53] Only a being that is ultimately worthy is deserving of worship. A God with limitations is surely not ultimately worthy. Only an infinite Being is deserving of worship.

Third, evil does not prove that God must be limited.[54] An all-good and all-powerful God may choose to allow evil and human suffering for the purpose of a greater good. What exactly this greater good may entail in specific cases may remain a mystery to finite beings, but, the wisdom of an infinite Being far transcends the wisdom of finite beings (Isaiah 55:8-9). A child may question the decision of his parents to allow him to receive surgery. But he does not have access to the amount of information that his parents have, and he does not see that the present pain he is enduring is for the purpose of future healing. The relationship of mankind to God is analogous to the relationship of this child to his parents. Also, God may defeat evil in the future (as the Bible teaches). In fact, only an infinite God can guarantee the ultimate defeat of evil. A finite God cannot.[55]

In short, finite godism leaves one with a god who is no God at all. For he, like the rest of the universe, needs a cause. He is not worthy of worship, and he cannot guarantee the defeat of evil. A god who needs help and forgiveness deserves only sympathy, not worship.

POLYTHEISM

Polytheism is the world view that teaches the existence of more than one god.[56] Many Eastern religions accept the existence of many gods. This includes certain forms of Hinduism, Confucianism, Shintoism, Taoism, and Jainism.[57] Western thought is itself not without polytheistic belief systems. Ancient Greek mythology expressed polytheistic themes.[58] Several cult groups such as Mormonism, Scientology, and the Unification Church spread polytheism in the West today.[59]

Polytheism fails for the following reasons. Either all the gods are finite or at least one of them is infinite. They cannot all be finite. If they are all finite beings, then they would need an infinite Being to ground their existence, but, then this infinite Being would be God.[60]

So there must exist at least one infinite Being. It is not possible that there exist more than one infinite Being. If more than one infinite Being existed, they would limit one another's existence. One infinite Being could prevent the other infinite Being(s) from accomplishing its goals. But then these beings would not be infinite since they would be limited by another's power. Therefore, there must exist one, and only one, infinite Being.[61] This one infinite Being would alone be God. Therefore, Polytheism fails in its attempt to explain reality.

SKEPTICISM NOT A VIABLE OPTION

All world views, except for theism, have been shown to be failures. They are self-contradictory and fail to explain the available evidence. If theism, the only remaining world view, also fails, then skepticism would be the only possible alternative. However, skepticism also fails.

If one decides to be a skeptic, then he has chosen to suspend judgment on all things. He has failed to suspend judgment on his choice to be a skeptic.[62] This, of course, is contradictory. Also, no one can consistently live like a skeptic. For example, if someone suspended judgment on what he should eat, then he would eventually starve to death.[63]

CONCLUSION

Therefore, since skepticism fails as all non-theistic world views have failed, then, due to the process of elimination, theism must be true. Still, the following chapters will include a positive defense of theism.

ENDNOTES

[1] Norman L. Geisler and William D. Watkins, *Worlds Apart* (Grand Rapids: Baker Book House, 1984), 38.

[2] Geisler, *Apologetics*, 263.

[3] Geisler and Watkins, 98-99.

[4] Geisler, *Apologetics*, 173-174.

[5] Geisler and Watkins, 78-79.

[6] Ibid., 94.

[7] Ibid., 98.

[8] Ibid., 96.

[9] Ibid., 99.

[10] Geisler, *Apologetics*, 187.

[11] Ibid., 239.

[12] Ibid.

[13] Ibid., 241.

[14] Craig, 81-93.

[15] Ibid., 81.

[16] Ibid., 93.

[17] Geisler, *Apologetics*, 247-249.

[18] Ibid., 247-248.

[19] Walter Martin, *The New Age Cult* (Minneapolis: Bethany House Publishers, 1989), 65.

[20] Ibid.

[21] Geisler, *Apologetics*, 247-248.

[22] Geisler and Watkins, 102.

[23] Ibid., 108.

[24] Ibid.

[25] Ibid., 136.

[26] Ibid.

[27] Millard J. Erickson, *Christian Theology* (Grand Rapids: Baker Book House,

1985), 272.

[28] Geisler and Watkins, 139.

[29] Erickson, 735.

[30] Geisler and Watkins, 21.

[31] Geisler, *Apologetics*, 208-209.

[32] Ibid., 147-148.

[33] Ibid.

[34] Ibid.

[35] Ibid., 148.

[36] Ibid., 181.

[37] Ibid.

[38] Ibid., 182.

[39] Ibid., 181.

[40] Ibid.

[41] Ibid., 148.

[42] Ibid., 181.

[43] Ibid., 188.

[44] Ibid.

[45] Ibid., 189-190.

[46] Ibid., 188.

[47] Ibid.

[48] Harold S. Kushner, *When Bad Things Happen to Good People* (New York: Avon Books, 1981), 148.

[49] Ibid., 134.

[50] Ibid., 147-148.

[51] Geisler and Watkins, 211-212.

[52] Ibid., 212.

[53] Ibid.

[54] Ibid., 212-213.

[55] Ibid., 212.

[56] Ibid., 217.

[57] Ibid., 218.

[58] Ibid.

[59] Ibid.

[60] Norman Geisler, *Thomas Aquinas* (Grand Rapids: Baker Book House, 1991), 130.

[61] Ibid.

[62] Geisler and Feinberg, 93-94.

[63] Ibid., 94.

CHAPTER 6

The Ontological Argument

H aving refuted atheism and other non-theistic world views, it is now time to defend theism. The following four chapters will discuss several philosophical arguments for the existence of the God of theism. In this chapter the ontological argument for God's existence will be examined.

The ontological argument for God's existence is an attempt to prove God's existence solely from the idea or concept of God.[1] It is an attempt to prove God's existence from reason alone. No appeal to the facts of experience is considered. In this way the ontological argument differs from other arguments for God's existence.

All other arguments for God's existence argue from something in existence to the existence of God. The teleological argument argues from the design in the universe to the existence of an intelligent Designer.[2] The moral argument argues from the existence of moral values to the existence of the absolute moral Lawgiver.[3] The cosmological argument reasons from the existence of dependent beings to the existence of a totally independent Being.[4] Only the ontological argument argues from the concept of God to His existence. The ontological argument alone does not begin with the facts of experience.

The ontological argument was originated by Anselm of Canterbury (1033-1109 AD). Various forms of this argument have been defended throughout history by great thinkers such as Rene Descartes (1596-1650), Benedict Spinoza (1632-1677), Gottfried Wilhelm Leibniz (1646-1716). Charles Hartshorne, Norman Malcolm, and Alvin Plantinga are three twentieth century scholars who have also defended this argument.[5] But, the ontological argument has also been opposed throughout history by other great thinkers such as Gaunilo (a contemporary of Anselm), Thomas Aquinas (1225-1274), David Hume (1711-1776), and Immanuel Kant (1724-1804).[6] In short, the ontological argument has been one of the most hotly debated issues in the history of philosophy.

ANSELM OF CANTERBURY

In Anselm's work entitled *Proslogium*, he introduced this unique argument for God's existence. Though Anselm himself may not have been aware of the fact, he actually gave two different versions of the ontological argument.[7]

In Anselm's first argument, he stated that both believers and unbelievers define God as the greatest conceivable

Being. Anselm reasoned that if God does not exist, then a person could conceive of a being greater than the greatest conceivable Being. A person could conceive of a being who had the same attributes as the greatest conceivable Being, but also existed. But, then this would be the greatest conceivable Being. Therefore, concluded Anselm, the greatest conceivable Being must exist.[8]

Another way of stating this first argument is that the greatest conceivable Being would be, by definition, a being who has every possible perfection. Since Anselm held that existence itself is a perfection, he concluded that the greatest conceivable Being must exist.[9]

Anselm's second form of the ontological argument stated that God, by definition, is a necessary Being. A necessary Being is a being that cannot not exist. Therefore, reasoned Anselm, it is a contradiction to say that a necessary Being does not exist. Hence, concluded Anselm, since God is a necessary Being, He must exist.[10]

OBJECTIONS TO THE ONTOLOGICAL ARGUMENT

In Anselm's own lifetime his ontological argument was opposed by a monk named Gaunilo.[11] Gaunilo's main attack on the ontological argument was found in his illustration of a perfect island. Gaunilo reasoned that we have just as much right in concluding that God exists merely from our idea of a perfect Being as we do in concluding the existence of a perfect island solely from our idea of a perfect island.[12] Anselm responded by stating that the analogy between a perfect island and a perfect Being breaks down. For the idea of a perfect island does not include its existence, while the idea of a perfect Being does entail its existence.[13] Anselm accused Gaunilo of not understanding what Anselm's argument was actually saying. Today, many philosophers agree that Gaunilo misunderstood Anselm's argument.[14]

Still, this does not mean that Anselm's ontological argument cannot be refuted. Immanuel Kant believed that Anselm's argument was fallacious. Kant stated that the deficiency of Anselm's argument was in Anselm's view that existence is a perfection.[15] The concept of God as a Being who has all perfections does not entail the *existence* of that Being because existence is not a perfection. Existence does not change the concept of a being, it merely posits actual existence to that being. To say that something has existence is to say that it actually exists outside the mind. The concept of a perfect Being who exists is no greater than the concept of a perfect Being who does not exist. They are both the same concept, though one has existence while the other does not. Therefore, as far as Kant was concerned, it is faulty reasoning to go from the realm of pure thought to the realm of actual existence by treating existence as one of the perfections that the most perfect Being must have.[16]

From Kant's time on, this has become the primary objection to the ontological argument.[17] Still, many philosophers who agree with this criticism believe that it only applies to the first type of Anselm's ontological argument. They believe that Anselm's second argument remains intact despite Kant's critique. Two of these philosophers are Charles Hartshorne and Norman Malcolm.[18]

RESTATEMENTS OF THE
ONTOLOGICAL ARGUMENT

Norman Malcolm defended Anselm's second type of ontological argument. Malcolm reasoned that the existence of a necessary Being can either be necessary (it cannot not exist), impossible (it cannot exist), or possible (it may or may not exist). Malcolm stated that since no one has shown the concept of a necessary Being to be contradictory (logically impossible), then the existence of a necessary Being is possible. If it is possible for a necessary Being to exist, then it must exist. It is a contradiction to say that a being which cannot not exist (a necessary Being) may or may not exist. Therefore, a necessary Being must exist.[19] The heart of Malcolm's argument can be stated as follows. By definition, a necessary Being cannot not exist. Therefore, a necessary Being must exist.[20]

However, Malcolm admits a weakness in his argument. He concedes that he is unaware of any way to prove that there is no contradiction in the concept of a necessary Being. Therefore, it is logically possible that the concept of a necessary Being is contradictory. Hence, it may be the case that it is impossible for a necessary Being to exist. Therefore, at best, Malcolm's ontological argument only shows that it is probable that a necessary Being exists. For it is always possible that someone will someday show that the concept of a necessary Being is contradictory.[21]

Another modern restatement of the ontological argument comes from Alvin Plantinga.[22] After years of examining and critiquing the ontological argument, Plantinga proposed his own version of the argument. Though Plantinga viewed Anselm's argument as problematic, Plantinga considers his own argument as valid.[23]

Plantinga argued that the greatest possible Being would have to be a being that exists as the greatest possible Being in every possible world. Plantinga concludes that since the actual world is a possible world (it is not an impossible world), then the greatest possible Being must exist in the actual world.[24]

Though Plantinga's argument appears valid, it ceases to be an ontological argument. Its premises leave the realm of pure reason by assuming the existence of the actual world.[25] By definition, an ontological argument must prove God's existence from the mere concept of God. Other arguments for God's existence begin with something that actually exists and then argue to the existence of God. Plantinga's argument should be classified as a type of cosmological argument. It starts with the existence of the actual world and then argues to God's existence.[26]

Christian philosophers Norman Geisler and Winfried Corduan consider this the downfall of the ontological argument. For it is always logically possible that nothing exists.[27] Therefore, in order for the ontological argument to work, it must start with the premise, "something exists."[28] But, then it is no longer an ontological argument. It starts with actual existence, not pure thought.

CONCLUSION

An examination of Anselm's ontological argument has produced several observations. First, most philosophers believe that Immanuel Kant has successfully refuted Anselm's first argument. Second, Norman Malcolm's version of Anselm's second ontological argument leaves the realm of logical necessity since he admits he cannot prove that the concept of a necessary Being is not an impossible being. In other words, Malcolm admits that it is possible that someone will someday prove that the concept of a Necessary Being involves a contradiction. Therefore, his argument, if successful, could only prove that God probably exists. And, third, Plantinga showed that the only apparent way to rescue the ontological argument is to begin with the cosmological premise that something exists. But, then the ontological argument is no longer ontological; it leaves the realm of pure reason.

Another factor should also be mentioned. Charles Hartshorne and Benedict Spinoza were mentioned earlier as proponents of the ontological argument. But they both denied the existence of a theistic God. Spinoza's God was a pantheistic God (a God who is identical to the universe).[29] Hartshorne utilized the ontological argument to prove the existence of a panentheistic God (a God whose body is the world).[30] Even if the ontological argument is valid (and it seems that it is not), it apparently does not reveal enough about God's nature to show us what kind of God He (or it) is.[31]

At best, apologists should suspend judgment on the ontological argument. At worst, it is a failure. Either way, defenders of the Christian faith should look elsewhere to provide evidence for God's existence.

ENDNOTES

[1] Craig, 61.

[2] Ibid., 66.

[3] Ibid., 70.

[4] Ibid., 62.

[5] Geisler and Corduan, 123-149.

[6] Ibid.

[7] Ibid., 123.

[8] Anselm, *St. Anselm: Basic Writings* trans. by S. N. Deane (Lasalle: Open Court Publishing, 1966), 7-8.

[9] R. C. Sproul, John Gerstner, and Arthur Lindsley, *Classical Apologetics* (Grand Rapids: Zondervan Publishing House, 1984), 102.

[10] Anselm, 8-9.

[11] Ibid., 145-153.

[12] Geisler and Corduan, 126.

[13] Ibid.

[14] Ibid., 126-127.

[15] Ibid., 134.

[16] Ibid., 134-135.

[17] Ibid., 135.

[18] Ibid., 142.

[19] Ibid., 142-144.

[20] Ibid., 143.

[21] Ibid., 144.

[22] Alvin C. Plantinga, *God, Freedom, and Evil* (Grand Rapids: Eerdmans Publishing Company, 1974), 85-112.

[23] Geisler and Corduan, 146.

[24] Plantinga, 108-110.

[25] Geisler and Corduan, 147-148.

[26] Ibid., 148.

27 Ibid.

28 Ibid.

29 Ibid., 149.

30 Ibid.

31 ;Ibid.

CHAPTER 7

The Teleological Argument

S ince the ontological argument appears to have failed in its attempt to prove God's existence through reason alone, Christian apologists must start with the *facts* of experience and argue to God's existence. The ontological argument tried to prove God's existence *a priori* (prior to and apart from experience).[1] It sought to establish God's existence as definitionally true. Rather than trying to deduce God's existence with logical necessity, defenders of the faith should argue inductively. Apologists must argue *a posteriori* (from the particulars of experience to God's existence).[2] Thus, they must aim for conclusions that are probable, though not rationally inescapable.

Inductive arguments argue from particulars to the whole.[3] They, unlike deductive arguments (which argue from the whole to the particular), do not bring conclusions that are logically necessary. Inductive arguments, at best, only bring conclusions that have a high degree of probability.[4] But this is no cause for alarm since almost all, if not all, of man's knowledge is based on probability.[5] The ontological argument (the only deductive argument for God's existence) has apparently failed. Therefore, Christian thinkers should argue inductively for God's existence.

Three of the best known inductive arguments for God's existence are the teleological, the moral, and the cosmological. This chapter will discuss the teleological argument, also known as the argument from design.[6]

ANCIENT GREEK PHILOSOPHERS

The teleological argument may be the oldest argument for God's existence.[7] Many ancient Greek philosophers reasoned that the the order in the universe could only be accounted for by the workings of an intelligent mind.[8] Plato agreed. He referred to God as the *Demiurge*, which means "hard worker."[9] Still, Plato's Demiurge differs from the God of the Bible. For the Demiurge designed the cosmos out of preexisting chaotic matter.[10] The Demiurge is the designer of the universe, but not the Creator (as He is in Christianity). Plato's student Aristotle also argued for the existence of a divine Being due to the design in the universe.[11]

THOMAS AQUINAS (1225-1274)

Thomas Aquinas, the great Christian theologian and philosopher of the thirteenth century, is famous for his five ways to prove God's existence.[12] In Aquinas' fifth way to prove God's existence, he argued that some things in nature work towards certain goals despite the fact that they have no knowledge.[13] But things without knowledge do not move towards a goal unless guided by something which has knowledge. Aquinas reasoned that just as an arrow requires an archer, so too everything in nature is guided towards its goal by someone (God) with knowledge.[14]

WILLIAM PALEY (1743-1805)

William Paley is famous for his "watch-maker argument."[15] This is probably the best known teleological argument. Paley stated that if a person who had never seen a watch before were to find one in the wilderness, he would conclude that it was a product of intelligent design.[16] He would see that its several parts were put together for the purpose of producing motion. This motion is so well regulated that it is able to mark the time of the day with precision.[17] The person would see that if there were any small variation in the shape, size, or position of the many parts of the watch, there would either be no motion at all or motion that would not serve the purpose of keeping time.[18] The person would conclude that the watch must have a maker.[19]

Paley then looked at nature and saw evidence of design similar to that of the watch, but to a greater degree.[20] He reasoned that there must be an intelligent Designer of the universe.

Paley's argument is thought to have been refuted by David Hume, but, this does not appear to be the case. Paley wrote his argument thirty years after Hume's supposed refutation was published.[21] The watch-maker argument is not vulnerable to the majority of Hume's criticisms.[22]

HUME'S CRITICISMS OF
THE TELEOLOGICAL ARGUMENT

David Hume (1711-1776) raised objections against the teleological argument for God's existence in his work *Dialogues Concerning Natural Religion*. Several of his objections will be mentioned here. First, Hume reasoned that the Designer of the universe would not have to be infinite. Since the universe is finite, its Designer needs only to be finite.[23] However, if Hume was right and the Designer is only finite, then this Designer would also need a Designer. Eventually one would have to arrive at an infinite Designer. Otherwise, there would be no explanation for the design in the universe. For an infinite regress of designers is impossible (this point will be established in the chapter on the cosmological argument).

Second, Hume speculated that since there is evil in the world, one would be justified in assuming that the Designer of the world is Himself evil.[24] The Christian could here argue that evil exists merely as a privation of that which is good.[25] Hence, for a being to be totally evil, it would have to be non-existent.[26] Therefore, it would be impossible for there to exist an infinite evil being.

Third, Hume reasoned that since ships are designed by multiple designers, the universe may have been designed by multiple designers.[27] Proponents of the teleological argument respond to this criticism by simply emphasizing the unity found in the universe. For it is more probable that this unity is caused by one Designer rather than several designers.[28]

There is evidence that Hume himself did not find these and other objections to the teleological argument unanswerable. The closing paragraph of Hume's *Dialogues Concerning Natural Religion* implies that he found the teleological argument to be more probable than the objections he raised.[29] Hume's point seems to be that the case for Christianity based upon the teleological argument does not have a rationally certain conclusion.[30] Still, he does express respect for this argument.

MODERN SCIENCE AND THE TELEOLOGICAL ARGUMENT

It should also be noted that recent advances in modern science have strengthened the teleological argument.[31] Science has uncovered that the highly complex information found in the genetic code of living organisms is similar to that of human language. Since human language is known to have been produced by intelligence, it is reasonable to conclude that living organisms were themselves produced by an intelligent Being.[32]

CONCLUSION

Defenders of the faith need to recognize that the case for Christian theism does not rest solely on the teleological argument.[33] Rather, a combination of other arguments with the teleological argument strengthens the case for Christianity.[34] In fact, the objections to the teleological argument can be easily answered by utilizing the cosmological argument at the outset to prove the existence of one uncaused Cause of all else that exists.[35] Then the teleological argument can be used to show that this uncaused Cause must also be an intelligent Being.[36] Therefore, the teleological argument does have a useful, though supplementary, role in proving the existence of the God of the Bible.[37]

ENDNOTES

[1] Geisler and Feinberg, 288.

[2] Ibid.

[3] Ibid., 57-58.

[4] Ibid.

[5] Ibid., 129-131.

[6] Craig, 66.

[7] Ibid.

[8] Ibid.

[9] Sahakian, 54.

[10] Ibid., 55.

[11] Ibid., 70-71.

[12] Saint Thomas Aquinas, *Summa Theologiae*. ed. Timothy McDermott. (Westminster: Christian Classics, 1989), 13-14.

[13] Ibid., 13.

[14] Ibid., 14.

[15] Craig, 68.

[16] William Paley, *Natural Theology: Selections*. ed. F. Ferre (Indianapolis: Bobbs Merrill, 1963), 3-4.

[17] Ibid.

[18] Ibid.

[19] Ibid.

[20] Ibid., 13.

[21] Craig, 68.

[22] Ibid.

[23] Geisler and Corduan, 98.

[24] Ibid.

[25] Saint Augustine, *City of God.* 22.[1.]

[26] Geisler, *Thomas Aquinas*, 154-155.

[27] Geisler and Corduan, 98.

[28] Moreland, *Scaling the Secular City*, 65.

[29] David Hume, *Dialogues Concerning Natural Religion* (New York: Hafner Publishing Company, 1948), 95.

[30] Moreland, 65.

[31] Geisler and Corduan, 104.

[32] Ibid.

[33] Moreland, 65.

[34] Ibid.

[35] Geisler, *Apologetics*, 247-249.

[36] Ibid.

[37] Ibid.

CHAPTER 8

The Moral Argument

The moral argument for God's existence reasons from the existence of universal moral values to the existence of a universal moral Lawgiver.[1] This argument maintains that the source of the objective moral values we experience must be an ultimately good Being.[2]

The apostle Paul stated that Gentiles, who do not have God's written Law, "show the work of the Law written in their hearts, their conscience bearing witness, and their thoughts alternately accusing or else defending them" (Romans 2:15). The Bible declares that God has written His Law on the hearts of all men. This is the basis for defenders of the faith using moral arguments for God's existence.

THOMAS AQUINAS

Aquinas' fourth way to prove God's existence is his argument from the different degrees of perfection found in finite things.[3] Men commonly judge some things to be more perfect than other things. But judgment concerning the degree of perfection in things only makes sense if there exists a most perfect Being. To say that something is more perfect than something else is to say that it more closely approximates the perfect. One cannot determine that something falls short of a perfect standard unless that perfect standard is known. Therefore, the perfect must exist. Whatever contains the most perfection must be the source of all the perfection that exists in other beings. Therefore, concludes Aquinas, there must exist a most perfect Being who is the cause of all the perfections that exist in beings containing lesser degrees of perfection.[4]

IMMANUEL KANT

Immanuel Kant rejected any attempts to prove God's existence through pure rational argumentation. However, he believed that God's existence must be practically posited in order to make sense of man's moral experience.[5] Kant argued that man must assume the existence of God and life after death if he is to make sense of his desire for happiness and his moral duty.[6] Kant believed that the uniting of man's desire for happiness with man's moral duty could not occur in this life or without God's power. Therefore, reasoned Kant, it is morally necessary (not rationally necessary) to assume God's existence.[7]

It must be remembered that this argument does not prove God's existence. It only states that man must assume God's existence and the afterlife if he is to make sense of his moral life. Kant's argument does not demand that we conclude that God exists; it merely says that man must live as if God does in fact exist.[8]

C. S. LEWIS (1898-1963)

C. S. Lewis used an advanced form of the moral argument for God's existence in his work *Mere Christianity*.[9] Lewis argued that man's idea of right and wrong is a clue to the meaning of the universe.[10] Lewis reasoned that there must exist a universal moral law for several reasons. First, all moral disagreements between persons imply an appeal to a standard of behavior to which all persons are subject.[11] People accused of doing wrong usually claim that their action did not violate the universal standard, or that they somehow had a special excuse for not submitting to the standard in this particular case.[12] They do not usually deny the standard itself. Second, quarreling often occurs when one person tries to prove that the action of another person is wrong. However, the fact that two people quarrel about whether or not an action was moral implies that they agree that there is such a thing as right and wrong.[13] One person claims the action was right; the other person claims the action was wrong. What they agree upon is the *concept* of right and wrong (the moral law).[14]

Lewis reasons that this moral law could not be mere herd instinct. If it were, then the stronger instinct would always win, but, this is not the case. Often, man suppresses his stronger instinct in order to do what he thinks is right.[15] For instance, when confronted with imminent danger, a man may desire to run for safety but instead chooses to disregard his own well-being to rescue another. Therefore, the moral law is not man's basic instincts. Instead, it judges between these instincts to determine which instinct is to be applied in the specific situation.[16]

Lewis also believed that it is wrong to say that this moral law is merely a social convention.[17] For not everything that man has learned from others is a social convention. Some things, like mathematics, would be true even if it was never taught.[18] The moral law is like mathematics in this respect. It is real regardless of what one's society teaches about it.[19] Social progress makes no sense unless the moral law exists independent of societies.[20] If the moral law is merely invented by society, then one society (America) cannot call the actions of another society (Nazi Germany) wrong.[21]

Lewis declared that the moral law cannot be a law of nature.[22] For a law of nature is descriptive. It describes how nature is, how it usually acts. But, the moral law does not describe how nature is. The moral law is prescriptive; it prescribes how nature ought to be.[23] The moral law stands above man and judges his behavior.

Lewis concluded that there exists a moral law above all men to which they are subject.[24] However, matter could not be the cause of moral laws.[25] Matter gives instructions to no one. Experience shows us that mind is the cause of moral laws.[26] Therefore, this universal moral law that stands above all men must come from a Mind that stands above all men.[27]

CONCLUSION

Each of the three thinkers mentioned in this chapter have

contributed valuable aspects to the moral argument. Lewis' argumentation is impressive. A person might arbitrarily deny the existence of the moral law, but the denial is forced and temporary. If that person is wronged, he will appeal to the moral law for justice.

If the moral law is merely subjective, then no one can declare the actions of another to be wrong. If the moral law is produced by nations, then no nation can condemn the actions of another nation. The moral law could not even be the product of world consensus. The world consensus of the twentieth century could not condemn the slavery of the nineteenth, first, or any other century since world consensus favored the practice of slavery during those times.

The moral judgments of men do not make sense unless the moral law stands above all individuals, all nations, and any supposed consensus of the world. The moral law is universal; it applies to all mankind. The moral law is also eternal; it does not change with time. Therefore, there must exist an eternal moral Lawgiver who stands above all men. Prescriptive laws only come from lawgivers.

A variation of Kant's argument can be utilized effectively by apologists. If there exists no God who will someday judge the actions of men, then it makes no difference how one now lives. One million years from now it will make no difference if one lived like Mother Theresa or Adolph Hitler. If God does exist, then how one lives does make a difference. If there is life after death with rewards and punishment, then the moral experience of man makes sense.

Finally, the thought of Aquinas can be used. When a man makes moral judgments he determines some things to be more perfect than other things. This implies the knowledge of something which is the ultimately perfect standard by which all else is judged. No one can determine a line to be crooked without knowledge of a straight line. The Christian believes that this ultimately perfect standard is the all-good God Himself. Without this all-good God, there could be no such thing as evil. For evil is merely the perversion of that which is good. There could be nothing that is good unless there exists an ultimately good Being who is the source of all lesser goods.

Despite the apparent strengths of the moral argument for God's existence, it is susceptible to some of the same criticisms as the teleological argument. Could not there be several moral lawgivers instead of one? Maybe the moral lawgiver is only a finite being.[28] Though these objections can be answered, premises from the cosmological argument for God's existence must be utilized to do so.[29]

Therefore, it is probably best to start one's argument for God's existence with cosmological premises. This will provide evidence for the existence of one Being who is the eternal uncaused cause of all else that exists. Then one can use premises from the moral and teleological arguments to show that this one Being must also be a moral and intelligent Being.

ENDNOTES

[1] Geisler and Corduan, 94.

[2] Craig, 70.

[3] Geisler, *Thomas Aquinas*, 121.

[4] Ibid.

[5] Geisler and Corduan, 109.

[6] Ibid., 109-110.

[7] Ibid., 110.

[8] Ibid.

[9] C. S. Lewis, *Mere Christianity* (New York: Collier Books, 1952), 15-39.

[10] Ibid., 15.

[11] Ibid., 17.

[12] Ibid.

[13] Ibid., 17-18.

[14] Ibid.

[15] Ibid., 22-23.

[16] Ibid., 23.

[17] Ibid., 24.

[18] Ibid.

[19] Ibid.

[20] Ibid., 24-25.

[21] Ibid., 25.

[22] Ibid., 27-29.

[23] Ibid., 28.

[24] Ibid., 31.

[25] Ibid., 34.

[26] Ibid.

[27] Ibid.

[28] Geisler and Corduan, 121-122.

[29] Ibid.

CHAPTER 9

The Cosmological Argument

The cosmological argument for God's existence reasons for the existence of God from the existence of the universe or some being in the universe.[1] This argument begins with the facts of experience and concludes that there must be a cause or reason to explain these facts.

There are three distinct types of cosmological arguments. Thomas Aquinas (1225-1274) used the argument based on the principle of existential causality (all limited, dependent existence needs a cause for its continuing existence).[2] Bonaventure (1221-1274) used the kalaam cosmological argument (everything that has a beginning needs a cause).[3] Gottfried Wilhelm Leibniz (1646-1716) utilized the principle of sufficient reason (everything that exists must have an adequate explanation for why it exists).[4]

AQUINAS: EXISTENTIAL CAUSALITY

Thomas Aquinas is famous for his five ways to prove God's existence.[5] In his first way, he argued from the observable movement or change in the universe to the existence of an unmoved Mover. Aquinas' second way reasons that the the causality found in the universe demands the existence of a first, uncaused Cause. His third way concludes with the existence of an independent Being as the cause for the continuing existence of all dependent beings.[6] These first three ways to prove God's existence are cosmological arguments. They all use the principle of existential causality.

Aquinas' fourth and fifth ways to prove God's existence are not cosmological arguments. Aquinas' fourth way (the limited perfections in other beings must be caused by the existence of a most perfect Being) could be classified as a moral argument. His fifth way (the fact that mindless nature moves toward specific goals implies the need for an intelligent Mind to guide these natural processes) is a teleological argument.[7]

As stated above, Aquinas' first three ways to prove God's existence utilize the principle of existential causality. The thrust of these three arguments is as follows. Aquinas argues that experience shows man that limited, dependent beings exist. These limited, dependent beings need other beings for their continued existence. For example, humans and animals depend on air, water, and food to sustain their existence. However, Aquinas argues that adding limited, dependent beings together will never produce an unlimited and independent whole. Therefore, the sum total of limited, dependent beings (the universe) is itself limited and dependent.

Hence, concludes Aquinas, the ultimate cause of the continuing existence of all limited, dependent beings must itself be unlimited and independent.[8]

Aquinas further argues that there cannot be two or more unlimited and independent beings because, if there were, they would limit one another's existence. But then they would not be unlimited. Therefore, there can only be one unlimited and independent Being.[9]

Aquinas reasoned that this unlimited and independent Being must have all its attributes in an unlimited way. Otherwise, it could not be an unlimited Being.[10] Therefore, this Being must be all-powerful, for He is the source of all the power in the universe.[11] No other power can limit Him. He must be eternal for He is not limited by time.[12] He must be immaterial since He is not limited by matter.[13] This Being must also be all-good since He is not limited by evil.[14] He must also be unlimited in knowledge.[15]

As was mentioned in an earlier chapter, the teleological and moral arguments can be used to compliment the cosmological argument. Therefore, Aquinas' fifth way to prove God's existence (his teleological argument) can be used to provide additional information about the unlimited and independent Being. Since mindless nature works towards goals (such as acorns always becoming oak trees and not something else), there must be an intelligent Designer overseeing natural processes. For without intelligent design and guidance, nature's processes would be left to chance. There would be no orderly patterns that could be described as natural laws. Therefore, this unlimited and independent Being that all finite and dependent existence depends upon for its continued existence, must be an intelligent Being.[16]

Christian philosopher Norman Geisler is a modern proponent of Aquinas' cosmological argument using the principle of existential causality.[17] Winfried Corduan, another contemporary Christian philosopher, also employs this type of cosmological argumentation in his writings.[18]

BONAVENTURE: THE KALAAM COSMOLOGICAL ARGUMENT

Saint Bonaventure utilized the kalaam cosmological argument for God's existence.[19] Bonaventure argued that whatever began to exist must have a cause. He believed that it could be proven that the universe had a beginning. Therefore, concluded Bonaventure, the universe must have a Cause.[20]

Both Bonaventure and Aquinas believed that the universe had a beginning. They accepted this because it was taught in the Bible. However, Aquinas did not believe that this could be proven philosophically. Bonaventure disagreed. He believed that it could be philosophically proven that the universe had a beginning. Therefore, Aquinas argued for the sustaining Cause of the universe (existential causality) while Bonaventure argued for the Cause for the beginning of the universe (the kalaam argument).[21]

Bonaventure contended that if the universe had no beginning, then there would exist an actual infinite set of events in time. However, Bonaventure reasoned that an actual infinite set is impossible. If an actual infinite set were possible, then contradictions would be generated, and contradictory situations cannot be true. For example, let's say that there are two sets of numbers. Set A contains all the even numbers. It is therefore infinite. But, Set B contains all the even and odd numbers. Set B would then contain twice as many members as Set A; still, Set A and Set B are equal because they are both infinite. Thus, the contradiction is evident. Bonaventure did not deny potential infinite sets. He only denied infinite sets of *actual* things (such as actual events in time).[22]

Bonaventure also concluded that since it is impossible to traverse an actual infinite set, then the universe could not be eternal. It had to have a beginning. If the universe is eternal, then one could never reach the present moment. For no matter how many moments one passes, one will never pass an infinite set of moments. But, if the universe is eternal, then there are an infinite set of moments in the past. Hence, one would not be able to reach the present moment. But, since mankind has reached the present moment, it is proof that the universe had a beginning.[23]

In addition to this philosophical evidence, there is now strong scientific evidence for the beginning of the universe as well. Though this evidence was not available in Bonaventure's day, it can be used by the contemporary apologist to strengthen or confirm Bonaventure's cosmological argument. Scientific evidence for the beginning of the universe includes the second law of thermodynamics (energy deterioration) and the big bang model.[24]

The second law of thermodynamics is one of the most firmly established laws of modern science.[25] It states that the amount of usable energy in the universe is running down.[26] This means that someday in the finite future all the energy in the universe will be useless. In other words, if left to itself, the universe will have an end.[27] If the universe is going to have an end, it had to have a beginning.[28] At one time, in the finite past, all the energy in the universe was usable. This would mark the beginning of the universe. However, the universe is "winding down"; therefore, it must have originally been "wound up." [29] Hence, the universe is not eternal; it had a beginning. Since it had a beginning, it needs a cause. For from nothing, nothing comes.[30]

The big bang model also teaches that the universe had a beginning.[31] In 1929, astronomer Edwin Hubble discovered that the universe is expanding at the same rate in all directions.[32] As time moves forward, the universe is growing apart. This means that if one goes back in time the universe would be getting smaller and smaller. Eventually, if one goes back far enough into the past, the entire universe would be what scientists call "a point of infinite density." [33] This marks the beginning of the universe, the big bang.[34]

There have been two main attempts by modern scientists to refute the beginning of the universe. The first is the steady state model.[35] This view holds that the universe had no beginning. Instead, it always existed in the same state. However, this view (which never gained wide acceptance in modern times) was disproven in 1965 when the radiation background of the universe was discovered. This radiation background indicated that the universe was at one time in an extremely hot and dense state. Thus, the universe has not existed throughout all eternity in a steady-state.[36]

The second attempt to escape the beginning of the universe is the oscillating model.[37] This model teaches that at some point during the universe's expansion, gravity will halt

the expansion and pull everything back together again. From
that point there will be another big bang. This process will
be repeated over and over again throughout all eternity.[38]
But the oscillating model fails. First, there is no known principle of physics that would reverse the collapse of the universe into another big bang.[39] Second, current scientific
research has shown that the universe is not dense enough for
gravity to pull it back together again.[40] Third, even if it
could be proven that several big bangs have occurred, the
second law of thermodynamics would still require that there
was a first big bang.[41] Therefore, since the universe had a
beginning, it needs a cause.

What if the cause of the universe needs a cause? Could not
an infinite chain of causes and effects exist stretching back-
wards in time throughout all eternity? The answer is no. It
has already been shown that an actual infinite set is impossible. There had to be a first Cause. This first Cause must be
uncaused. It could not be caused by another, for then it would
not be the first Cause. Nor could it be self-caused because it
is absurd to say that a being preexisted its own existence in
order to cause its own existence.[42] Therefore, only an eternal,
uncaused Cause can be the cause of the universe.

Again, the teleological and moral arguments for God's
existence can be utilized to complete the cosmological argument. Since intelligent life is found in the universe, the Cause
of the universe must be an intelligent Being. No one has ever
shown how intelligence could have evolved from mindless
nature.[43] Intelligence cannot come from non-intelligence.[44]

Morality also exists in the universe. Without morality,
there would be no such thing as right and wrong. However,

the moral judgments people make show that they believe in the objective reality of right and wrong,[45] but nature is non-moral.[46] No one holds a rock morally responsible for tripping him. Since nature is non-moral but morality exists in the universe, the Cause of the universe must be a moral Being.[47]

If morality is relative, then each person can decide for himself what is right and what is wrong,[48] and no one can condemn the brutal actions of Adolph Hitler. Society also cannot be the cause of moral laws since societies often pass judgment on one another.[49] Therefore, one society, when judging another society, appeals to a moral authority that transcends all societies. Only an absolute moral Lawgiver who is qualitatively above man and societies can be the cause of a moral law that stands above man and societies and judges their actions. Therefore, the uncaused Cause of the universe must be an intelligent and moral Being. This means that God must be a personal Being.[50]

LEIBNIZ: SUFFICIENT REASON

Gottfried Wilhelm Leibniz utilized the principle of sufficient reason to argue for the existence of God.[51] This principle states that there must be a sufficient reason or explanation for everything that exists.[52] Many beings exist that do not contain in themselves the reason for their existence. For instance, a man depends on his parents for his birth, and he needs air and food for his continuing existence.[53] Leibniz argued that there cannot be an infinite regress of explanations because then there would be no explanation why anything exists at all.[54] Therefore, reasoned Leibniz, something must exist which contains within itself the reason for its own existence.[55] This Being explains not only its own existence but the existence of all else as well.

Leibniz is not claiming that God is self-caused; this would be absurd. Instead, he is claiming that God is self-explained. God is the explanation for His own existence only because He is an uncaused Being.[56]

FINDING COMMON GROUND

The cosmological argument for God's existence (in any of its three forms—existential causality, kalaam, sufficient reason) is probably the strongest argument for God's existence.[57] Still, non-Christians often reject that it proves God's existence. Yet, the apologist is not attempting to prove God's existence with mathematical certainty. In fact, very little (if anything) can be known with mathematical certainty about the real world.[58] One can, however, argue to God's existence from premises that are beyond reasonable doubt.[59] The denial of these premises is absurd, forced, and temporary.[60] The premises can be viewed as actually undeniable (each premise must be affirmed in any attempt to deny it).[61] Therefore, God's existence can be proven with a high degree of probability.

Probability arguments can be extremely convincing. The everyday decisions that man must make are rarely (if ever) based on certainty. They are instead based upon a high degree of probability. When a person drives over a cement bridge extended hundreds of feet above the ground, that person is expressing faith that the bridge will support the weight of his vehicle. This is not a blind and irrational faith. There is much evidence for man's ability to build such structures. The person driving across the bridge is basing his faith on the available evidence though absolute certainty eludes him. In like manner, the existence of God can be proven with a high degree of probability. Because man is limited in knowledge and vulnerable to errors, his knowledge is limited and therefore extends only to the realm of probability.

It should also be noted that a person may know (with a high degree of probability) something to be true, though he or she may not be able to prove it.[62] A suspect of a crime may know he is innocent yet not be capable of proving it. In the same way, many Christians know (with a high degree of probability) that God exists, though they cannot prove that He does.

Having said this, it is now necessary to show that the basic premises of the cosmological argument are beyond reasonable doubt. Once this is shown to be the case, the apologist and the non-theist will share common ground from which the apologist can argue for God's existence.[63]

This common ground (which forms the premises for the cosmological argument) consists of four factors, 1) the law of non-contradiction, 2) the law of causality, 3) the principle of analogy, and 4) the basic reliability of sense perception.[64] All people, whether theist or atheist, must live like these four principles are true.

The law of non-contradiction states that something cannot be both true and false at the same time and in the same way.[65] If something is true, then its opposite must be false. If the non-theist attempts to deny the law of non-contradiction, he must first assume it to be true in order to make the denial. Otherwise, the opposite of the denial could also be true.[66] Though a person may deny this law, he must live, speak, and think as though it is true.[67]

The law of causality states that everything that has a beginning needs a cause.[68] To deny this law is absurd. If the law of causality is not true, then something could be caused to exist by nothing. However, nothing is nothing. Therefore, nothing can do nothing. Hence, nothing can cause nothing. From nothing, nothing comes. If one rejects the law of causality, then there is no basis for modern science. Modern science must assume this law when attempting to discover the relationships that exist between the elements of the universe.[69]

The principle of analogy declares that two effects which are similar often have similar causes.[70] For instance, a watch shows tremendous design and complexity.[71] So does the universe. In fact, a single celled animal has enough genetic information to fill an entire library.[72] Therefore, it seems reasonable to conclude that since it takes an intelligent being to make a watch, it must also have taken an intelligent being to design the universe. It seems rather unlikely that an entire library's worth of information could have evolved by chance. An Intelligent designer is needed.

Finally, the basic reliability of sense perception is accepted by theists and non-theists alike.[73] Though people are sometimes mistaken in the conclusions they draw from what their senses perceive, their sense perceptions can usually be trusted. All people live as though their sense perceptions were reliable. They move when rocks are thrown at them. People stay clear of railroad tracks when they hear the whistle of a coming train. Modern science must assume the basic reliability of sense perception in order to examine nature.

Any strong cosmological argument will be built upon
these four presuppositions (the laws of non-contradiction,
causality, analogy, and the basic reliability of sense perception). Though the non-theist may deny these four presuppositions for sake of argument, he must presuppose them in
everyday life. He must live as if they were true. Any philosophy that cannot be lived, such as is the case with atheism,
is not worth believing. Though a person may verbally deny
God's existence, he must still live as if the God of the Bible
does in fact exist.[74]

FIVE FINAL POINTS

First, after examining the theistic arguments, it is evident
that the strongest philosophical argument for God's existence is some type of cosmological argument. However, this
does not mean that the other arguments for God's existence
have no place in apologetics. As was shown in this chapter,
the moral and teleological arguments can be used very successfully to complete the cosmological argument.[75]
Premises from the moral and teleological arguments can be
used to unveil some of the attributes of the uncaused Cause.

Second, when using the kalaam cosmological argument
(as was utilized by Bonaventure), the Christian apologist
should not argue against the existence of an actual infinite
set. For the Christian believes that God is all-knowing
(omniscient). This is usually understood to mean that God
knows an actual infinite number of things. Therefore, an
actual infinite set does exist (though only in the mind of

God). Hence, the Christian apologist is incorrect when he argues against the existence of an actual infinite set. The kalaam argument for God's existence loses no force by merely arguing for the impossibility of traversing an actual infinite set (this is all that Zeno's paradox proves). That would be enough to prove that the universe had a beginning and, therefore, needs a Cause. Or, the apologist may argue for the impossibility of an actual infinite set existing outside the mind of an infinite God.[76]

Third, when doing apologetics, the Christian should adapt his or her argumentation to meet the personal needs of the listener. For some non-theists, psychological arguments for God's existence will be more persuasive. For others, philosophical arguments are more convincing. The goal of apologetics is to lead people to Christ. Therefore one's apologetics should be tailored to meet the needs of the listener.

Fourth, all defenders of the faith must remember that even if their argumentation is effective, the listener may still choose to suppress the truth. It is not easy for people to admit that there exists a God to whom they must answer. The desire for human autonomy (to be one's own master) is very strong. Only the inward persuasion of the Holy Spirit, working in this case with apologetic argumentation, can convince the human will to accept the existence of the God of the Bible.[77]

Fifth, arguments for God's existence provide strong evidence for the existence of the theistic God. Still, historical evidences are needed to show that Christianity is the true theistic faith (as opposed to Islam and the present-day form of Judaism).[78]

ENDNOTES

[1] Craig, 62.

[2] Ibid., 63.

[3] J. P. Moreland, *Scaling the Secular City*, 18.

[4] Craig, 65.

[5] Aquinas, 12-14.

[6] Ibid., 12-13.

[7] Ibid., 13-14.

[8] Ibid., 12-13.

[9] Ibid., 25.

[10] Geisler, *Thomas Aquinas*, 125.

[11] Aquinas, 60-61.

[12] Ibid., 23-24.

[13] Ibid., 20-23.

[14] Ibid., 19-20.

[15] Ibid., 39-40.

[16] Ibid., 13-14.

[17] Geisler, *Apologetics*, 237-258.

[18] Winfried Corduan, *Reasonable Faith* (Nashville: Broadman and Holman Publishers, 1993), 102-121.

[19] Moreland, 18.

[20] Frederick Copleston, *A History of Philosophy* vol. II, (New York: Image Books, 1985), 251-252.

[21] Ibid., 262-265.

[22] Ibid., 263.

[23] Ibid., 264.

[24] Craig, 81, 88.

[25] Moreland, 34.

[26] Norman L. Geisler and J. Kirby Anderson, *Origin Science* (Grand Rapids: Baker Book House, 1987), 117.

27 Moreland, 35.

28 Ibid.

29 Ibid.

30 Ibid., 38.

31 Craig, 81-82.

32 Peacock, 83-85.

33 Craig, 82.

34 Ibid., 82-83.

35 Ibid., 83.

36 Ibid.

37 Ibid.

38 Ibid., 84.

39 Ibid.

40 Ibid., 86.

41 Ibid., 90.

42 Geisler, *Apologetics,* 246.

43 Francis A. Schaeffer, *Trilogy* (Wheaton: Crossway Books, 1990), 283.

44 Geisler, *Apologetics*, 247.

45 C. S. Lewis, *Mere Christianity*, 19.

46 Ibid., 26-29.

47 Geisler and Corduan, 112.

48 Ibid., 113.

49 Ibid.

50 Geisler, *Apologetics*, 249.

51 Copleston, *A History of Philosophy*, vol. IV, 324.

52 Geisler and Corduan, 164.

53 John Hick, *The Existence of God*, 168-169.

54 Geisler and Corduan, 164.

55 Ibid.

56 Copleston, *A History of Philosophy*, vol. IV, 325.

57 I disagree with Geisler and Corduan on this point. They consider only the

Thomistic cosmological argument using the principle of existential causality as successful. I find the arguments put forth by Geisler and Corduan against both the kalaam argument and the use of the principle of sufficient reason unconvincing. See Geisler and Corduan, *Philosophy of Religion*, 172-174.

[58] Geisler and Feinberg, 129-131.

[59] Ibid., 87-88.

[60] Charles Hodge, *Systematic Theology vol. I*, (Grand Rapids: Eerdmans Publishing Company, 1989), 210.

[61] Geisler, *Apologetics*, 239.

[62] Moreland, 245.

[63] Sproul, Gerstner, and Lindsley, 70-72.

[64] Ibid.

[65] Ibid., 72-82.

[66] Ibid.

[67] Ibid.

[68] Craig, 74-75.

[69] Sproul, Gerstner, and Lindsley, 82.

[70] Geisler and Anderson, 69, 124.

[71] Hick, 99-104.

[72] Geisler and Anderson, 162.

[73] Sproul, Gerstner, and Lindsley, 71-72.

[74] Schaeffer, *Trilogy*, 78-79.

[75] Geisler, *Apologetics*, 247-249.

[76] I discussed the rejection of this premise ("the impossibility of an actual infinite set") in a November, 1994, telephone conversation with Dr. J. P. Moreland, professor of philosophy at the Talbot School of Theology. Moreland used this premise in his book *Scaling the Secular City*. Moreland agreed that it is probably best to no longer use this premise in the kalaam cosmological argument, and that the premise "the impossibility of traversing an actual infinite set" would be sufficient in establishing the beginning of the universe. Dr. Moreland also related that the premise of the kalaam argument could be changed to "the impossibility of an actual infinite set in the concrete (outside the mind) realm." This premise could be proven by showing the contradictions that would arise if actual infinite sets existed outside the mind. Some of these contradictions have already been discussed in this chapter. What the Christian should not argue for is the impossibility of an actual infinite set existing in the abstract (inside a mind) realm. For if an actual infinite set cannot exist in a mind, then God cannot know an actual infinite number of things. But, if an actual infinite set exists in a mind, this mind

would have to be an infinite Mind (an omniscient mind). Only an infinite Mind can know an infinite number of things. Since it is impossible to traverse an actual infinite set, finite minds will never know everything an infinite Mind knows even if the finite mind continues to learn more and more throughout eternity. Also, the impossibility of traversing an actual infinite set shows that God (the infinite Mind) did not attain His knowledge of an infinite number of things by learning them one idea at a time. Instead, God knows an infinite number of things in one eternal glance or thought.

[77] Craig, 18-27.

[78] Geisler, *Christian Apologetics*, 263-265.

CHAPTER 10

The Problem of Evil

O ne of the greatest obstacles keeping people from accepting Christ is the problem of evil.[1] This problem can take several different forms. First, the metaphysical problem of evil asks how evil can exist in a world created by an all-good God.[2] Is God the cause of evil, or, is evil itself uncreated and eternal? Maybe evil is not real. Maybe it is simply an illusion.[3] The metaphysical problem deals with the origin and reality of evil in God's universe.

Second, the moral problem of evil deals with the evil choices of personal beings.[4] This form of the problem argues that since an all-good God would want to destroy evil, and an all-powerful God is able to destroy evil, the existence of evil proves that no all-good, all-powerful God exists.[5] The Christian apologist defends the existence of an all-good and all-powerful God. Therefore, he will respond to this argument.

The third form of the problem of evil is called the physical problem of evil.[6] The physical problem of evil deals with incidents of natural disasters and innocent humans suffering.[7] How could God allow evil to occur that is not directly caused by the abuse of human free will?[8]

The fourth and final form of the problem of evil is not really a philosophical issue. It is the personal problem of evil.[9] The personal problem of evil is not a theoretical question about the existence of evil. Instead, it is a personal struggle with a traumatic experience in one's own life.[10] Examples of this would be the sudden and unexpected death of a loved one, a bitter divorce, the loss of a job, or the like. In these situations, the troubled person does not need philosophical answers. What is needed is encouragement, comfort, and biblical counsel.[11] Since this form of the problem of evil does not deal with philosophical discussion, it will not be dealt with in this chapter. The remainder of this chapter will deal with the first three forms of the problem of evil.

THE METAPHYSICAL PROBLEM OF EVIL

The metaphysical problem of evil can be stated as follows: 1) God created everything that exists, 2) evil exists, 3) therefore, God created evil.[12] There are several ways people respond to this argument. First, like the Christian Science Cult, some choose to deny the reality of evil.[13] They view evil as an illusion, but this entails a rejection of Christian Theism which clearly accepts the real existence of evil and offers Christ as its solution.[14] Therefore, viewing evil as an illusion is not an option for the Christian apologist.

A second possible response to the metaphysical problem is dualism. This is the view that God and evil are coeternal.[15] In this view, God did not create evil since evil is eternal. This view fails in that it makes evil a second ultimate being along with God. God would then no longer be infinite since He and evil would limit each other. However, the cosmological argument has shown that there must be an infinite Being to explain and ground all finite existence. There cannot be two infinite beings, for they would limit each other. If God and evil are both finite, then there would have to be an infinite cause for the existence of both. Dualism would only push the problem of evil further back. It does not offer any ultimate solution to the dilemma. Also, the acceptance of dualism entails a rejection of the existence of the God of the Bible. Therefore, it is not an option for the Christian theist.[16]

The Christian apologist must defend the reality of evil without proposing evil as eternal or as a creation of God.[17] Saint Augustine dealt with this same problem centuries ago. His proposed solution to the metaphysical problem of evil was that all things created by God are good. Nothing in its created nature is evil. Evil, therefore, cannot exist solely on its own. However, evil is real; it does exist. Still, it must exist in something good. Evil is a privation, a lack or absence of a good that should be there. Evil is a corruption or perversion of God's good creation. Blindness in a man is evil, for God created man to see. But, blindness in a rock is not evil, for God never meant rocks to have sight. Evil, according to Augustine, is a lack of a good that should be there. Augustine stated, "evil has no positive nature; what we call evil is merely the lack of something that is good."[18]

Augustine stated that God did not create evil; He merely created the possibility for evil by giving men and angels free will. When men and angels exercised their free will by disobeying God, they actualized the possibility for evil.[19]

Thomas Aquinas argued against the metaphysical problem of evil along the same lines as did Augustine.[20] This basic response has been the traditional Christian solution to the metaphysical problem of evil. God did not create evil, but, evil exists as a privation or corruption of that which is good. God cannot be blamed for evil. He is only responsible for creating the possibility of evil. When God gave angels and men free will, He created the possibility of evil. Fallen angels and fallen men are responsible for evil through their abuse of free will.[21]

THE MORAL PROBLEM OF EVIL

The moral problem of evil affirms that an all-good God would want to destroy evil, while an all-powerful God is able to destroy evil. Since evil exists, it is concluded that an all-good, all-powerful God does not exist.[22] Some people respond by denying God's existence (atheism). Others deny that God is all-powerful (finite godism). Rabbi Harold Kushner is an example of the latter. He argues that God is not all-powerful. Kushner declares that mankind needs to forgive God for His failures and help Him to combat evil.[23] Obviously, the options of atheism and finite godism are not viable for Christians. Christians must defend both God's omnipotence (all-powerfulness) and His infinite goodness. Therefore, the moral problem of evil must be answered in another way. Christian philosophers Geisler and Corduan offer several effective responses to the moral problem of evil.

First, there is an unnecessary time limit placed on God.[24] The argument against the existence of the theistic God from moral evil assumes that because evil exists God cannot be both all-good and all-powerful. However, what if an all-good and all-powerful God allowed evil for the purpose of a greater good? What if this God is also in the process of destroying evil and will someday complete the process?[25]

Second, God may have created the possibility of evil for the purpose of a greater good (human and angelic free will). God would not force His love on angels or mankind, for any attempt to force love on another is rape (and not really love at all).[26] Therefore, He gave men and angels the freedom to accept or reject His love and His will. Free will necessitates the possibility of evil coming into the universe.[27] In fact, human and angelic free choices brought evil and human suffering into the world.

Third, God will use evil for good purposes. If evil did not exist, there could be no courage, for there would be nothing to fear. If evil did not exist, man could only love his friends; he could never learn to love even his enemies. Without evil, there would be no enemies.[28] Only an infinite God can know all the good He will bring out of evil (Isaiah 55:8-9).

Fourth, Geisler and Corduan argue that an all-good and all-powerful God is not required to create the best possible world. They reason that all He can be expected to do is create the best possible way to achieve the greatest possible world. Heaven is the greatest possible world.[29]

Several other points could also be made. First, the atheist usually denies the existence of objective evil since he knows that this would admit to the existence of the absolute moral law.[30] The atheist knows that once he acknowledges the absolute moral law, the existence of God (the absolute moral law Giver) surely will follow.[31] For evil to be objectively real, it must exist as a perversion of that which is ultimately good. To escape this conclusion, the atheist usually chooses to deny the existence of evil. Therefore, it is rather ironic that the atheist (who usually denies the existence of evil) attempts to use evil to disprove the existence of the God of the Bible. The presence of evil may be problematic for all other world views (including Christian theism), but it is totally devastating to atheism. If there is no God, then there are also no objective moral values. The most consistent atheists, such as Nietzsche, have readily admitted this.[32]

Second, all world views must deal with the problem of evil, but the God of the Bible is the only guarantee that evil will ultimately be defeated.[33] The God of deism is no longer concerned with the problems of this world (such as evil).[34] In pantheism, evil is an illusion.[35] In atheism, there is no basis to call anything evil.[36] But, the biblical God guarantees that evil will be defeated through Christ's death, resurrection, and return (John 1:29; 1 Peter 2:24; 3:18; Romans 4:25; Isaiah 9:6-7; 11:1-9; Zechariah 9:9-10; Revelation 20;4-6).

Third, non-Christians act as if the existence of evil is an unexpected factor in the Christian world view, but this is not the case. God would not have given mankind the Bible had it not been for the problem of evil. If man had not fallen into sin in the garden, he would have had no need for salvation (Genesis 3:1-7; Romans 3:10, 23; 5:12; 6:23). The Bible could actually be titled "God's Solution to the Problem of Evil."

In short, the solution to the moral problem of evil (how an all-good, all-powerful God can co-exist with evil) is that God gave humans and angels free will. It is the abuse of this free will by humans and angels that has brought evil and human suffering into existence. God created the possibility for evil (by giving man and angels free will), not evil itself.

Christian philosopher Alvin Plantinga adds an important detail concerning the Christian response to the moral problem of evil. He writes that there are two ways Christians can respond to this dilemma. First, he may develop a free will theodicy. A theodicy is an attempt to explain what was God's reason (or reasons) for allowing evil. On the other hand, according to Plantinga, the Christian does not have to go that far. Instead of presenting a free will theodicy, he may develop a free will defense. In this case, rather than attempting to explain the reason as to why God allows evil and human suffering, the Christian can merely suggest a *possible* reason why God has allowed evil and human suffering.[37] The free will defense, according to Plantinga, is sufficient in itself to show that the existence of evil does not rule out the possible existence of the God of theism.[38]

In other words, since the problem of evil is an attempt to prove God's existence as being impossible, the Christian only needs to provide possible solutions to this problem. Once this is done, God's existence will have been shown to be possible. Further argumentation (such as the cosmological, teleological, moral, and ontological arguments) can then be presented to argue for God's existence with a higher degree of probability.[39]

THE PHYSICAL PROBLEM OF EVIL

The physical or natural problem of evil deals with evil not directly connected to the abuse of human freedom.[40] All physical or natural evil is at least indirectly related to the abuse of human freedom. Without the Fall of man in history, creation would still be perfect (Genesis 1:31). Still, much physical evil is not directly related to human choices. Natural disasters such as earthquakes, floods, hurricanes, and deaths of innocent infants are examples of physical evil.

Geisler and Corduan list five explanations for physical evil.[41] None of the five are meant to be all-encompassing. Each explains some of the physical evil that occurs. First, some physical evil is necessary for moral perfection.[42] There can be no courage without something evil to fear. Misery is needed for there to be sympathy. Tribulation is needed for there to be endurance and patience.[43] For God to build these characteristics in man, He must permit a certain amount of physical evil.

Second, human free choices do cause some physical evil.[44] It would be an obvious error to assume that no physical evil is caused by the abuse of human free will. The choice to drink and drive has caused much physical evil. Many infants have been born with an addiction to cocaine due to their mothers' choice to abuse drugs while pregnant.

It is impossible for God to remove all physical evil without tampering with human free will.[45] It is even possible that some major natural disasters are caused by the evil choices of humans. According to the Bible, this was the case with Sodom and Gomorrah (Genesis 18:20-21; 19).

Third, some physical evil is caused by the choices of demons.[46] The Scriptures speak of demons (fallen angels led by Satan) causing suffering to humans (Job 1, 2; Mark 5:1-20). Demons oppose God and His plans, but they will ultimately be defeated by Christ (Revelation 19, 20, 21, 22).

Fourth, God often uses physical evil as a moral warning.[47] Physical pain is often a warning that greater suffering will follow if behavior is not changed. Examples of this would be excessive coughing that is often caused by smoking and heavy breathing caused by over training during a physical workout. Also, God may use pain and suffering to cause a person to focus on Him, rather than on worldly pleasures.[48]

Fifth, some physical evils are necessary in the present state of the physical world.[49] To survive, animals often eat other animals. Humans eat animals as well. It appears that, at least in the present state of the creation, lower life forms are subjected to pain and death in order to facilitate the preservation of higher life forms.[50]

Physical evil, therefore, does not present insurmountable problems for Christian theism. Though man is limited in knowledge and cannot infallibly ascertain why God allows each and every case of physical evil, the five reasons given above should suffice to show that the presence of physical evil in no way rules out the existence of the God of the Bible.

CONCLUSION

Once the Christian apologist has provided strong evidence for God's existence, he need only give possible reasons why an all-good and all-powerful God would allow evil and human suffering. God has good reasons for allowing evil and human suffering, even though we may not know them fully. Therefore, the existence of evil does not disprove the existence of an all-good and all-powerful God. These two are not mutually exclusive.

ENDNOTES

[1] Nash, 177.

[2] Geisler and Corduan, 318.

[3] Ibid.

[4] Ibid., 333.

[5] Ibid.

[6] Ibid., 364.

[7] Ibid.

[8] Ibid.

[9] Nash, 179-180.

[10] Ibid.

[11] Ibid., 180.

[12] Geisler and Corduan, 318.

[13] Mary Baker Eddy, *Science and Health with Key to the Scriptures* (Boston: The First Church of Christ, Scientist, 1971), 293, 447, 472, 480, 482.

[14] Geisler and Corduan, 318-319.

[15] Ibid., 319.

[16] Ibid., 319-320.

[17] Ibid., 318-320.

[18] Augustine, *City of God*, 11.9, 12.3, 14.11, 22.1.

[19] Geisler and Corduan, 323-324.

[20] Aquinas, 91-92.

[21] Geisler and Corduan, 320-330.

[22] Ibid., 333.

[23] Kushner, 129,134,145-148.

[24] Geisler and Corduan, 334.

[25] Ibid., 348.

[26] Ibid.

[27] Ibid.

[28] Ibid.

[29] Ibid., 342-343.

[30] C. S. Lewis, *Mere Christianity*, 34-39.

[31] Ibid.

[32] Friedrich Nietzsche, *The Portable Nietzsche*, ed. by Walter Kaufmann, (New York: Penguin Books, 1982), 228.

[33] Geisler and Watkins, 41.

[34] Ibid., 148-149.

[35] Ibid., 99-100.

[36] Ibid., 59.

[37] Plantinga, 28.

[38] Ibid.

[39] Ibid.

[40] Geisler and Corduan, 364.

[41] Ibid., 372-378.

[42] Ibid., 372-373.

[43] Ibid., 372.

[44] Ibid., 373.

[45] Ibid., 373-374.

46 Ibid., 375.
47 Ibid., 376.
48 Ibid.
49 Ibid.
50 Ibid., 376-378.

CHAPTER 11

Miracles

═══════════════════════

Christianity is a religion based in history. The claims, death, and resurrection of Jesus of Nazareth occurred in history. For this reason, historical apologetics is of great importance. If one can prove that Jesus really did rise from the dead in history, then one will have gone a long way towards establishing Christianity as the true religion. However, before an apologist can engage in presenting historical evidences for the resurrection of Christ, he must first answer the philosophical objections against the possibility of miracles. If miracles are by definition impossible, then it makes no sense to look into history to see if Jesus really rose from the dead.

The strongest philosophical argumentation against miracles came from the pens of Benedict Spinoza (1632-1677) and David Hume (1711-1776). Spinoza was a pantheist.[1] He believed in an impersonal god that was identical to the universe. He reasoned that an impersonal god could not choose to perform miracles, for only personal beings make choices. Whatever an impersonal god does, it must do by necessity. Spinoza believed that nature necessarily operates in a uniform manner. Therefore, he argued that the laws of nature cannot be violated. Since miracles would be violations of the laws of nature, they are impossible.[2]

David Hume was a deist. He believed that after God created the universe, He no longer involved Himself with His creation. Hume reasoned that miracles, if they occur, are very rare events. On the other hand, the laws of nature describe repeatable, everyday occurrences. Hume argued that the wise man will always base his beliefs on the highest degree of probability. Since the laws of nature have a high degree of probability while a miracle is improbable, Hume considered the evidence against miracles always greater than the evidence for miracles. Therefore, according to Hume, the wise man will always reject the proposed miracle.[3]

RESPONSE TO SPINOZA

Spinoza argued that miracles are impossible. Several things should be mentioned in refutation of Spinoza's argument. Though it is true that a pantheistic god cannot choose to perform a miracle (a pantheistic god is impersonal and, therefore, cannot choose anything), there is strong evidence that a pantheistic god does not exist.[4] As the cosmological argument has shown, a theistic God exists.[5] A theistic God is a personal God, and a personal God *can* choose to perform miracles.

Second, Spinoza's premise that the laws of nature can never be violated is suspect. The laws of nature are descriptive; they are not prescriptive. In other words, the laws of nature describe the way nature usually acts. The laws of nature do not prescribe how nature must act.[6]

Third, Spinoza's definition of a miracle as a violation of the laws of nature is objectionable. It is possible that miracles do not violate the laws of nature; they merely supersede the laws of nature. C. S. Lewis argued along these lines.[7]

Fourth, if God created the universe, then the laws of nature are subject to Him. God can choose to suspend or violate (depending on how one defines a miracle) the laws of nature any time He wishes. In short, Spinoza has failed to show that miracles are impossible.

RESPONSE TO HUME

Hume, unlike Spinoza, did not argue for the impossibility of miracles. Instead, he argued that miracles were so unlikely that the evidence against them will always be greater than the evidence for them. Hume argued that miracles are improbable, and that the wise man will only believe that which is probable. Hence, the wise man will never accept evidence for a miracle.[8]

The Christian apologist can respond to Hume's reasoning in the following manner. Just because usual events (the laws of nature) occur more often does not mean that the wise man will never believe that an unusual event (a miracle) has occurred.[9] The wise man should not *a priori* rule out the possibility of miracles. The wise man will examine the evidence for or against a miracle claim, and base his judgment on the evidence. Since there were over 500 witnesses who claimed to have seen Jesus risen from the dead (1 Corinthians 15:3-8), a wise man would not reject the miracle of the resurrection merely because all other men have remained dead. It seems that a wise man would examine a miracle claim if there are reliable eyewitnesses. If there is no good reason to reject the testimony of reliable eyewitnesses, it seems that a wise man would accept their testimony that a miracle has occurred.

CONCLUSION

Some people will not accept any event unless it has a natural cause. Therefore, they reject miracles because they have a supernatural Cause (God).[10] But, the cosmological argument has shown that the universe itself needs a supernatural Cause (God). Therefore, if there is a God who created the universe, then He would have no problem intervening in His universe by supernaturally working miracles within it. A person cannot rule out miracles simply because his world view does not allow them. If his world view is weak (such as pantheism and deism), then he has weak reasons for rejecting miracles. If, on the other hand, a person has strong evidence for his world view (such as theism), and that world view is consistent with the reality of miracles, then he has strong reasons for believing that miracles are possible.

This chapter has only shown that miracles are possible. Historical evidence must be examined to see whether miracles have actually occurred or not. Philosophical argumentation can only show that miracles are possible. Historical evidences must be utilized to determine if an alleged miracle (such as the resurrection of Jesus from the dead) has in fact occurred. Since the focus of this book is evidence for God's existence, argumentation for the historicity of Christ's resurrection will not be discussed.

ENDNOTES

[1] Norman L. Geisler, *Miracles and the Modern Mind* (Grand Rapids: Baker Book House, 1992), 18.

[2] Ibid., 15.

[3] David Hume, *An Inquiry Concerning Human Understanding* (New York: The Liberal Arts Press, 1955), 117-141.

[4] see Chapter 5 of this book.

[5] see Chapter 9 of this book.

[6] Terry L. Miethe, ed. *Did Jesus Rise From the Dead?* (San Francisco: Harper and Row, 1987), 18.

[7] C. S. Lewis, *Miracles* (New York: Collier Books, 1960), 59-60.

[8] Geisler, 23-28.

[9] Ibid., 27-31.

[10] Ibid., 50-51.

CHAPTER 12

Refuting Moral Relativism

P hilosophical apologetics often deals with the branch of philosophy called ethics. Ethics deals with issues of morality, that which is right and wrong.[1] The Christian ethical perspective holds to absolute moral values, laws that are universally binding. Often, non-Christian views hold to moral relativism. Moral relativism rejects the idea that there are objective rights and wrongs.[2] What is right for one person is not necessarily right for another person, and vice versa. Each person decides what is right for himself. Many atheists and pantheists are moral relativists.[3]

AN EXAMINATION OF MORAL RELATIVISM

Friedrich Nietzsche (1844-1900) was a German philosopher. He believed that the advances of human knowledge had proven that belief in God was a mere superstition. Nietzsche therefore reasoned that since "God is dead," all traditional values have died with Him. Nietzsche was angered with his atheistic colleagues who were unwilling to dismiss traditional moral absolutes which had no justification without God's existence.[4]

Nietzsche preached that a group of "supermen" must arise with the courage to create their own values through their "will to power." Nietzsche rejected the "soft" values of Christianity (brotherly love, turning the other cheek, charity, compassion, etc.); he felt they hindered man's creativity and potential. He recommended that the supermen create their own "hard" values that would allow man to realize his creative potential.[5] Nietzsche was very consistent with his atheism. He realized that without God, there are no universal moral values. Man is free to create his own values. It is interesting to note that the Nazis often referred to Nietzsche's writings for the supposed intellectual justification for their acts of cruelty.[6]

Many other atheists agree with Nietzsche concerning moral relativism. British philosopher Bertrand Russell (1872-1970) once wrote, "Outside human desires there is no moral standard."[7] A. J. Ayer believed that moral commands did not result from any objective standard above man. Instead, Ayer stated that moral commands merely express one's subjective feelings. When one says that murder is wrong, one is merely saying that he feels that murder is wrong.[8] Jean-Paul Sartre, a French existentialist, believed that there is no objective meaning to life. Therefore, according to Sartre, man must create his own values.[9]

There are many different ways that moral relativists attempt to determine what action should be taken. Hedonism is probably the most extreme. It declares that whatever brings the most pleasure is right. In other words, if it feels good, do it.[10] If this position is true, then there is no basis from which to judge the actions of Adolph Hitler as being evil.[11]

Utilitarianism teaches that man should attempt to bring about the greatest good for the greatest number of people.[12] Utilitarianism is problematic. First, "good" is a meaningless term if moral relativism is true, for then there would be no such thing as good or evil. Second, to say that man "should" do something is to introduce a universal moral command. However, there is no room for universal moral commands in moral relativism.[13]

Joseph Fletcher founded "situation ethics." Situation ethics is the view that ethics are relative to the situation. Fletcher claimed that he was not a moral relativist. He believed that there was only one moral absolute: love. Still, his concept of love was so void of meaning that his view of ethics, for all practical purposes, is synonymous with moral relativism.[14]

REFUTING MORAL RELATIVISM

The situation never determines what is right. It is God who determines what is right. Still, the situation may aid the Christian in finding which of God's laws should be applied.[15] For when two of God's commands come in conflict due to a situation so that a person cannot obey both, God requires that the person obey the greater command.

God then exempts the person from obeying the lesser command. An example of this is the fact that God compliments Rahab the Harlot for lying in order to save two innocent lives (Joshua 2; Hebrews 11:31; James 2:25).[16]

Moral relativists deny the absolute moral law. Still, they, like all people, recognize the evil actions of others when they are wronged. When they are wronged, they appeal to an objective and universal law that stands above man. Moral relativists deny absolute moral law in the lecture hall, but they live by it in their everyday lives.[17] Moral relativists reserve the right for themselves to call the actions of Hitler wrong,[18] but if there is no such thing as right and wrong (as the moral relativists say), they cannot really call any action wrong. The moral law does not ultimately come from within each individual, for then no one could call the actions of another evil.[19]

The moral law does not ultimately come from each society, for then one society could not call the actions of another society (such as Nazi Germany) wrong.[20] Finally, the moral law does not ultimately come from world consensus,[21] for world consensus is often wrong. World consensus once thought the world was flat. World consensus once considered slavery morally permissible.

Appealing to world or societal consensus as the ultimate source of the moral law is actually just an extension of the view that the individual is the ultimate source. The difference is only quantitative (the number of people increases). However, for there to be a moral law above all men (in order to judge all men), this moral law must be qualitatively above all men (not just quantitatively greater than the few). If there is an absolute moral law qualitatively above all men, all societies, and the world consensus, then there must be an absolute moral law Giver that stands qualitatively above all men, all societies, and world consensus.

The absolute moral law is eternal and unchanging. We use it to condemn the actions of past generations. Since the moral law is eternal and unchanging, the moral law Giver must also be eternal and unchanging. The moral law is not descriptive of what is; it is prescriptive of what should be.[22] Prescriptive laws need a Prescriber.

Since the absolute moral law leads directly to the existence of the theistic God (the absolute moral law Giver), many atheists and pantheists may feel compelled to reject its existence. Also, people who wish to live promiscuous lives often choose to reject God's existence. The apostle John appears to be talking about these people when he says:

> And this is the judgment, that the light is come into the world, and men loved the darkness rather than the light; for their deeds were evil. For everyone who does evil hates the light, and does not come to the light, lest his deeds should be exposed (John 3:19-20).

ENDNOTES

[1] Geisler and Feinberg, 24-26.

[2] Moreland, *Scaling the Secular City*, 240.

[3] Geisler and Watkins, 59, 99-100.

[4] Friedrich Nietzsche, 95-96, 143, 228.

[5] Ibid., 124-125, 139, 191, 197-198.

[6] Copleston, *A History of Philosophy*, vol. 7, 403.

[7] Russell, 62.

[8] Norman L. Geisler, *Christian Ethics* (Grand Rapids: Baker Book House, 1989), 32.

[9] Geisler and Feinberg, 406.

[10] Ibid., 400-401.

[11] Geisler, *Christian Ethics*, 36-37.

[12] Ibid., 63.

[13] Ibid., 73-75.

[14] Ibid., 43-61.

[15] Geisler and Feinberg, 411.

[16] Ibid., 424-427.

[17] Hodge, *Systematic Theology*, vol. 1, 210.

[18] Hick, *The Existence of God*, 183-186.

[19] Moreland, 246-247.

[20] Ibid., 243-244.

[21] Geisler and Feinberg, 355.

[22] C. S. Lewis, *Mere Christianity*, 27-28.

PART THREE

Scientific Apologetics

CHAPTER 13

The Scientific Case
For Creation

Today, many people believe that evolution is a biological fact. However, this is not the case. Science, by definition, deals with probabilities, not certainties. The next two chapters will explore the creation-evolution debate. This chapter will draw heavily upon the information found in the book *Origin Science* by Norman L. Geisler and J. Kirby Anderson.[1]

HISTORY OF THE
CREATION-EVOLUTION DEBATE

The creation model is the view that God created the universe without using evolution. The creation model dominated modern science before 1860.[2] Modern science was started by men who believed in the existence of the God of the Bible. Galileo, Isaac Newton, Francis Bacon, Johannes Kepler, and

Blaise Pascal are just a few who fit into this category.[3] Their belief in God's existence formed the foundation for modern science. They believed that a reasonable God created the universe in a reasonable way, so that through reason man could find out about the universe in which he lives.[4] In other words, the universe makes sense only because God designed it to make sense. Today, however, atheistic evolutionists have rejected this base for modern science.[5] They have rejected the existence of a reasonable God. But the question that they must face is this: "Without a reasonable God, can a person really expect the universe to make sense?"

The evolution model is the view that life spontaneously evolved from non-life without intelligent intervention.[6] The evolution model dominated modern science after 1860.[7] Charles Darwin published his book *The Origin of Species* around that time.[8] Darwin proposed a naturalistic explanation for the origin of the universe, first life, and new life forms.[9] He taught that nature can be explained without appealing to a supernatural origin. Darwin's proposal quickly became the predominant "scientific" view.

THE SCIENTIFIC METHOD

Evolution is not a scientific fact. The scientific method consists of six steps: 1) observation, 2) proposal of a question or problem, 3) hypothesis (an educated guess), 4) experimentation, 5) theory (a hypothesis with a high degree of probability), and 6) natural law (a theory thought to be valid on a universal scale).[10] Evolution is not a scientific law or theory, let alone a scientific fact. The supposed evolutionary changes from one species to another cannot be observed.[11] They supposedly occurred in the past. Therefore, since observation is the initial step in the scientific method, evolution cannot be proven through the scientific method.

The creation view is in the same category as evolution. Creation, scientifically speaking, is not a fact, law, or theory. Like evolution, the supposed creation is a singular event in the past. It cannot be observed. Therefore, both creation and evolution are only *scientific models*; they represent different ways to interpret the same evidence.[12]

This does not mean that creation and evolution cannot claim to be scientific. Contrary to popular belief, the scientific method is not the only way to search for truth in the field of science. Forensic science (crime scene investigation) does not use the scientific method, for the crime can no longer be observed. Still, forensic science is a legitimate science.[13] Science can be separated into two main divisions: operation science and origin science. Operation science deals with the repeatable; it is science of the observable present. It uses the scientific method. Forensic science, creation, and evolution do not fall into this category.[14] Origin science, on the other hand, deals with the non-repeatable; it deals with the singular events of the past. Origin science does not utilize the scientific method since singular events of the past can no longer be observed.[15] Forensic science, creation science, and evolutionary science fall into this category.

ORIGIN SCIENCE

Since the non-repeatable events of the past cannot be

observed, origin science does not make use of the scientific method. Instead, origin science uses the principles of analogy (also called uniformity) and causality to determine whether or not a model is plausible.[16] The principle of analogy states that when a scientist observes a cause bringing about a certain effect in the present, he should posit the same kind of cause for a similar effect in the past.[17] In other words, similar effects usually have similar causes. The principle of causality states that every event must have an adequate cause.[18] A scientist should use these two principles to determine the plausibility (or lack of plausibility) of a particular model.

Since the creation model and the evolution model fall under the heading of origin science, the principles of analogy and uniformity must be applied to them to determine which model is more plausible. It must be understood that the creation model and the evolution model both deal with the same evidence. An example of this is common anatomy. Common anatomy deals with the similarities in the body parts of different species. Examples of common anatomy are the similarities that exist concerning the arm of a man, the arm of an ape, the wing of a bird, and the fin of a shark. Both creationists and evolutionists agree to the common anatomy between different species of animal life. However, the two models interpret the evidence differently. The evolution model teaches that common anatomy proves common ancestry.[19] Common ancestry is the view that all species are related since one species has evolved into another. The creation model teaches that the same data (common anatomy) proves the existence of a common Designer. Animals often share common anatomy due to their being created and designed by the same God.[20]

Which model is more plausible? In order to answer this question, the principles of analogy and causality must be applied to the origin of the universe, the origin of first life, and the origin of new life forms. Both the creation model and the evolution model must be tested in these three areas to ascertain which model is more plausible.

THE ORIGIN OF THE UNIVERSE

Did the universe have a beginning, or did it always exist? This is a very important question. For if the universe had a beginning, it would need a cause. It could not have evolved into existence from nothing. If the universe is eternal then it may not need a cause. Fortunately, science is not silent on this question. The second law of thermodynamics is called energy deterioration. This law says that the amount of usable energy in the universe is running down.[21] Eventually, all the energy in the universe will be used up. This means that the universe is winding down. If it is winding down, it had to have been "wound up." If the universe is going to have an end, it had to have a beginning. There had to be a time when all the energy in the universe was usable; this marks the beginning of the universe.

The expansion of the universe and the big bang model also confirm the beginning of the universe.[22] In 1929, astronomer Edwin Hubble discovered that the universe is expanding at the same rate in all directions.[23] As time moves forward the universe is growing apart. This means that if one went back in time the universe would get denser. If one goes back in time far enough, the entire universe would be contained in what scientists have called "a point of infinite density." [24] But, a point can only be finitely dense. For a point to be infinitely dense it would have to be non-existent. Therefore, the universe came into existence from nothing a finite time ago.

There have been two main attempts to refute the proposition that the universe had a beginning. The first is the steady-state model. This view holds that the universe had no beginning. Instead, it always existed in the same state. However, because of the mounting evidence for the big bang model, this view has been abandoned by most of its adherents. [25]

The second attempt to evade the beginning of the universe is called the oscillating model. This model teaches that, at some point during the universe's expansion, gravity will halt the expansion and pull everything back together again. From that point there will be another big bang. This process will be repeated over and over again throughout all eternity. However, the oscillating model fails for three reasons. First, there is no known principle of physics that would reverse the expansion of the universe into another big bang. Second, current scientific research has shown that the universe is not dense enough for gravity to pull it back together again. Third, even if one could prove that several big bangs have occurred, the second law of thermodynamics would still require that there was a first big bang. [26]

Therefore, science has shown that the universe had a beginning, but, since from nothing, nothing comes, something must have caused the universe to come into existence.

Everything that has a beginning needs a cause. Since the universe needs a cause, the creation model is more plausible than the evolution model. If the universe were eternal, then the evolution model could claim some type of plausibility. But, for the above reasons, this is not the case. The universe is not eternal; it had a beginning. Something separate from the universe had to cause it to come into existence.

THE ORIGIN OF FIRST LIFE

Evolution teaches spontaneous generation—that life came from non-life without intelligent intervention.[27] However, spontaneous generation violates the law of biogenesis and the cell theory. The law of biogenesis states that "all living things arise only from other living things." [28] The cell theory defines the cell as the most basic unit of life, and declares that "new cells arise only from pre-existing cells." [29] Both the law of biogenesis and the cell theory are accepted by evolutionists; the evolutionists merely assume that first life is the exception to these principles. But, a model that violates scientific theories and laws should be abandoned. This is especially true when there is a rival model that does not violate scientific theories and laws.

The creation model posits the existence of an intelligent Being in order to bridge the gap from non-life to life. The creation model recognizes that the specified complexity (highly complex information) found in a single-celled animal could not be produced by chance. A single-celled animal has enough genetic information to fill one volume of an encyclopedia.[30] Just as an explosion in a print shop cannot randomly produce one volume of an encyclopedia, there is no way that a single-celled animal could have been produced by mere chance. Intelligent intervention was needed.[31]

Natural laws by themselves do not produce specified complexity. Geisler illustrates this point by stating that though natural laws can explain the Grand Canyon, they cannot explain the faces on Mount Rushmore.[32] The faces on Mount Rushmore reveal evidence of intelligent design.

Evolutionists often offer the Miller and Urey experiments as evidence that life has been produced from non-life in the laboratory. In response, several things should be noted. First, Chandra Wickramasinghe, one of Britain's most eminent scientists, calls these experiments "cheating." Miller and Urey start with amino acids, break them down, and then recover them. They do not produce something that wasn't there to begin with.[33] Second, Geisler states that the Miller and Urey experiments do not produce life. They only produce amino acids, which are the building blocks of life. Amino acids are to life what a single sentence is to one volume of encyclopedia.[34] Third, Geisler points out that even if these experiments did produce life from non-life in the laboratory (which they don't), it would support the creation model, not the evolution model. The reason for this is clear. The experiments would merely prove that to get life from non-life intelligent intervention (i.e., the scientists) is needed. The experiments would not prove that life spontaneously arose from non-life.[35]

Therefore, the creation model is more plausible than the evolution model when explaining the origin of first life. Intelligent intervention is necessary to produce life from non-life. It could not have happened by accident.

THE ORIGIN OF NEW LIFE FORMS

Many people believe that the fossil record proves evolution, but, this is not the case. In the fossil record, new life forms appear suddenly and fully developed.[36] There is no evidence of transitional forms (missing links). There are no fins or wings becoming arms. There are no intermediate forms. The gaps between forms in the fossil record are evidence against evolution, not for evolution.

Evolution teaches that single-celled animals eventually evolved into human beings. Of course, evolutionists claim this took long periods of time to be accomplished. A single-celled animal contains enough information to fill one volume of encyclopedia,[37] but the human brain contains enough information to fill twenty million volumes of encyclopedia.[38] Natural law, no matter how much time is involved, can never produce twenty million volumes of encyclopedia from one volume. Intelligent intervention is needed to produce more complex information.[39]

Evolutionists often point to mutations as the process by which evolution takes place.[40] However, mutations do not add more complex information to the genetic code. Instead, they merely garble the already existing genetic code.[41] For evolution to take place, new genetic information is needed. For example, single-celled animals would need new genes for the development of teeth, yet mutations produce no new genetic information.

Simple life forms do not go to complex life forms through

natural law alone.[43] Time plus chance plus natural laws can never produce more complex information.[44] Something must impart more information. Therefore, the creation model is more plausible than the evolution model concerning the origin of new life forms.

CONCLUSION

The scientific case for creation is very strong. Though it is true that creationists have never seen the invisible Creator, evolutionists also have never seen the supposed evolutionary changes of the past. The principles of analogy and causality support creationism as a superior model to evolution. Blind chance and natural laws are inadequate causes for the origin of the universe, first life, and new life forms. An intelligent Cause is needed in each case. The cause of the beginning of nature cannot be nature itself. No being can preexist its own existence in order to cause its own existence. Therefore, nature needs a supernatural Cause. This supernatural Cause must be an intelligent Being to bring life from non-life and complex life forms from simple life forms. Hence, the creation model is more plausible than the evolution model.

ENDNOTES

[1] Norman L. Geisler and J. Kirby Anderson, *Origin Science* (Grand Rapids: Baker Book House, 1987), entire book.

[2] Ibid., 37-52.

[3] Ibid.

[4] Ibid., 37-40, 51.

[5] Ibid., 52.

[6] Ibid., 82-86.

[7] Ibid.

[8] Ibid.

[9] Ibid.

[10] Tom M. Graham, *Biology, the Essential Principles* (Philadelphia: Saunders College Publishing, 1982), 6.

[11] Geisler and Anderson, 15.

[12] Ibid.

[13] Ibid., 25.

[14] Ibid., 36.

[15] Ibid., 127-132.

[16] Ibid.

[17] Ibid., 131-132.

[18] Ibid., 130-131.

[19] Morris, *Many Infallible Proofs*, 252-255.

[20] Ibid.

[21] Graham, 75.

[22] Craig, 81-83.

[23] Ibid., 82.

[24] Ibid.

[25] Ibid., 83.

[26] Ibid., 83-88.

[27] Morris, *Many Infallible Proofs*, 260.

[28] Graham, 18.

[29] Ibid., 12.

[30] Geisler and Anderson, 162.

[31] Ibid., 162-163.

[32] Ibid., 141.

[33] Varghese, 34.

[34] Geisler and Corduan, 105-106.

[35] Geisler and Anderson, 138-139.

[36] Ibid., 150-152.

[37] Ibid., 162.

[38] Ibid.

[39] Ibid., 163.

[40] Morris, *Many Infallible Proofs*, 256.

[41] Ibid.

[42] Charles Caldwell Ryrie, *You Mean the Bible Teaches That* . . . (Chicago: Moody Press, 1974), 111.

[43] Geisler and Anderson, 150.

[44] Scott M. Huse, *The Collapse of Evolution* (Grand Rapids: Baker Book House, 1983), 94.

CHAPTER 14

The Scientific Case
Against Evolution

The last chapter examined and defended the scientific case for creation. In this chapter, the scientific case against evolution will be discussed. There are major problems with the evolution model that render it obsolete as an explanation of the available scientific data. This chapter will comment briefly on these problem areas.

THERMODYNAMICS

Thermodynamics deals with the relationship between heat, energy, and work.[1] The first and second laws of thermodynamics pose serious problems for evolution. The first law of thermodynamics is called energy conservation. It states that the amount of energy in the universe remains constant; no energy is now being created or destroyed.[2] This means that if the universe had a beginning, whatever process or act that brought the universe into existence is no longer in operation today. In other words, the "creation process" is no longer operating today. Therefore, either the universe is eternal or the universe was created in the past; no continuing creative process is occurring.

The second law of thermodynamics is called entropy. Though the amount of energy in the universe remains constant, it changes form. The second law states that when energy changes form it becomes less usable.[3] Therefore, the amount of usable energy in the universe is running out. This means that the day will come when all the energy in the universe will have been used up. This will be the death of the universe. There must have been a time when all the energy of the universe was usable; this would be the beginning of the universe. In other words, since the universe is going to have an end, it is not eternal. If it is not eternal, then it must have had a beginning. The big bang model and the expansion of the universe also confirm the beginning of the universe.[4]

The evolutionist faces a dilemma. The first and second *laws* of thermodynamics together implicitly declare that the universe had a beginning. The evolutionists cannot deny these laws, for they are considered to be the most firmly established laws of modern science.[5] But, evolution runs counter to these two laws. When a scientific model contradicts a scientific law, the model should be abandoned. Since the first and second laws of thermodynamics teach that the universe had a beginning, then something outside the universe must have caused the universe to come into existence.

For, from nothing, nothing comes. Therefore, the universe could not have come into existence out of nothing.

EVOLUTIONARY DATING METHODS

The evolutionary dating methods are inconsistent and unreliable. All evolutionary dating methods are based upon uniformitarianism.[6] Uniformitarianism assumes that there were no world-wide catastrophes; therefore, the rate of decay has remained constant. Uniformitarianism assumes that today's processes have continued at the same rate throughout all time. However, if there were a world-wide flood and a special creation by God, then this uniformitarian assumption would be unwarranted.[7]

Evolutionary dating methods have been shown to be unreliable. Rocks known to have been only a few hundred years old have been dated to be hundreds of millions of years old.[8] Henry Morris has stated that there are many different ways to date the earth's age, but evolutionists only use those methods which give astronomically old dates since evolution needs millions of years to seem even slightly possible.[9] Two methods which point to a young earth are population statistics and the earth's magnetic field.[10] If one assumes the principle of uniformitarianism, then due to the present rate at which the population of mankind increases, the start of the present population would take one back 4,300 years to the traditional date for the flood.[11] Concerning the strength of the earth's magnetic field, if one assumes that the present rate of decay remains the same going back indefinitely into the past, then about 7,000 years ago it would have been too strong to sustain life.[12]

The most convincing argument for an old earth is probably that of the speed of light.[13] The speed of light is assumed by scientists to be constant. The light of distant stars and galaxies can be seen on earth. Since it would have taken billions of years for the light of some of these celestial bodies to reach earth (assuming the speed of light has remained the same throughout time), the universe must be billions of years old.[14] However, Barry Setterfield of Australia studied every measurement of the speed of light and concluded that the speed of light has not been constant throughout time; it was faster in the past. Setterfield's research, if reliable, reveals the age of the universe to be only 6,000 years old.[15] Still, Setterfield's research, for various reasons, has failed to convince many creation scientists (such as Hugh Ross), not to mention scientists who are evolutionists.[16]

Even if the universe is old, this would not refute the creation model. Many creationists believe in an old universe.[17] However, if the universe is young, the evolution model is destroyed. One thing is certain: the principle of uniformitarianism is an assumption that appears to go against the evidence. If uniformitarianism is true, then all the dating methods would reveal the same approximate dates. These dates would be old or young; they would not be old and young. Since some dating methods point to an old earth and others point to a young earth, the evolutionary dating methods are unreliable. Since uniformitarianism is not a given, the date of the universe is an open question.

THE FOSSIL RECORD

The fossil record is assumed to prove evolution, but, this is not the case. The fossil record shows no evidence of transitional forms (missing links). New life forms appear suddenly and fully developed.[18] There are no animals with half-fins or half-wings in the fossil record. If there were transitional forms, why have none been found? This is a serious problem for evolutionists. Harvard paleontologists Stephen Jay Gould and Louis Agassiz have admitted this lack of evidence for evolution in the fossil record.[19] Aggassiz, a nineteenth-century creationist, stated:

> Species appear suddenly and disappear suddenly in the progressive strata. . . . the supposed intermediate forms between the species of different geological periods are imaginary beings, called up merely in support of a fanciful theory.[20]

Gould, a twentieth century evolutionist, stated: "In any local area, a species does not arise gradually by the steady transformation of its ancestors; it appears all at once and 'fully formed.' " [21] It is interesting that the first geologists believed that the fossil record was evidence for the worldwide flood recorded in the Bible.[22] This view is strengthened by the fact that fossilization is extremely rare today. Even if the earth existed for millions of years, that would not be enough time for the present fossil record to have been produced without any world-wide catastrophes.[23] Fossilization is world-wide and caused by the rapid burial of

animals, which is something a world-wide flood would do.[24]
Another problem for evolution concerning the fossil
record is polystrate fossils. These are fossils that extend
through two or more layers of sedimentary rock.[25] These are
usually tree fossils. In order for a standing tree to be fossilized, it would have to be quickly buried before it decayed.
However, in these polystrate fossils, the several layers of
earth through which the tree extends supposedly took millions of years to form.[26] This reveals that evolutionists are
mistaken when they assume that layers of sedimentary rock
must take millions of years to form and therefore indicate
long periods of time. No tree can live for millions of years.
Therefore, these layers of sedimentary rock are not evidence
for an old earth. They must have been formed rapidly.[27]

Another problem for evolution is the fact that the fossil
record often appears out of sequence.[28] Sometimes "old"
fossils appear resting on rock layers containing "younger"
fossils.[29] The geologic column is "an imagined chronologi-
cal arrangement of rock units in columnar form with the presumed oldest units at the bottom and presumed youngest at
the top." [30] However, the world is full of strata appearing in
the wrong order.[31] If these layers took millions of years to be
formed as evolutionists say, then this would not be the case.

If one assumes the possibility that the fossil record was
formed rapidly, the world-wide flood offers the better explanation. The flood would tend to bury fossils in this order.
First, deep oceans creatures would be fossilized. Then, creatures in shallower water, followed by amphibians and land-
bordering creatures. Next would be swamp, marsh, and low
river-flat creatures (especially reptiles). After that, higher

mammals who retreated to higher ground in their attempt to escape the flood would be fossilized. Finally, humans would be overtaken.[32] This would be the "standard" order. However, due to upheavals in the earth's crust during and after the world-wide flood, there would be many exceptions.[33] A world-wide catastrophe such as the flood offers a much more plausible explanation for these exceptions than evolution does.[34]

Other interesting aspects of flood geology are the canopy theory and the global ice age. The canopy theory refers to Genesis 1:6-8.[35] In that passage, the Bible teaches that God surrounded the earth's atmosphere with a huge canopy of water. This would have worked liked the ozone layer does today. It would have filtered out poisonous rays from the sun, thus increasing longevity. This may explain why the Bible records pre-flood men living more than nine-hundred years (Genesis 5). After the flood, man's life-span would drastically decrease. The water contained in the canopy descended as rain and caused the great flood (Genesis 6:11-12) and covered the entire earth (Genesis 7:19). This would explain why three-fourths of the earth's surface is covered with water. In fact, if the earth were a completely smooth sphere, it would be covered by water 1.5 miles in depth.[36] After the flood, tremendous upheavals in the earth's crust due to the catastrophe would cause valleys to sink and mountains to rise (Psalm 104:5-9). The mountains that rose would become the dry land man now inhabits. The upheavals in the earth's crust could also explain much of the continental shifts that scientists have shown to have occurred.

A global flood would cause a global ice age.[37] Today,

evolutionists accept the global ice age, but they reject a universal flood which could have caused it. Because of this, glacial geologists have failed to determine what caused the ice age. Also, the lack of vegetation due to the ice age would have killed off most of the dinosaurs, though some recent dinosaur sightings are well-documented.[38]

LACK OF TRANSITIONAL FORMS

A devastating problem for the evolution model is the lack of transitional forms. No one possesses an undisputed missing link. All the supposed missing links between apes and men have been dismissed. Neanderthal Man and Cro-Magnon Man both have the features of modern man.[39] Colorado Man turned out to be a member of the horse family.[40] Java Man (also known as Pithecanthropus) was shown to be the remains of a large gibbon.[41] Heidelberg Man consisted of only a lower jaw.[42] Obviously, a lower jaw is insufficient evidence for a missing link. One can only speculate as to the makeup of the rest of the skull and skeleton. The Piltdown Man was revealed to be a clever hoax.[43] The Peking Man is now thought to be a large monkey or baboon.[44] The Southern Ape (also called Australopithecus), Dryopithecus, and Ramapithecus were extinct apes.[45] The East African Man (Zinjanthropus) was shown to be an ape.[46] Finally, the Nebraska Man, which consisted of only one tooth, was proven to be the tooth of an extinct pig.[47] This is rather interesting since this tooth had been presented as evidence in the 1925 "monkey trial" as "evidence" for the evolutionary model.[48] When the tooth of an extinct pig is mistaken for the tooth of the missing link between apes and men, it shows how subjective modern science has become. Though high school and college textbooks show drawings of the missing links from apes to men, the fact is that this art merely depicts the vivid imagination of scientists. No undisputed missing link between apes and men has been discovered.

Archaeopteryx was once thought to be a transitional form between reptiles and birds.[49] It had features resembling that of a reptile (teeth, lizard-like tail, and claws). But, archaeopteryx also had wings and feathers similar to a bird. Still, the archaeopteryx was fully developed. It did not have half-wings or the like. Archaeopteryx has now been classified as a bird. This is due to the fact that every characteristic of archaeopteryx can be found in some genuine bird, though some of its features are not found in reptiles.[50] It should also be noted that the supposed evolution of reptiles into birds is highly improbable. The lungs of a reptile have millions of tiny air sacs, while the lungs of birds have tubes. In order for a transitional form to exist between a reptile and a bird it would have to breathe without having fully-developed lungs,[51] and this is an impossibility.

An extinct, small three-toed animal called Eohippus was once thought to be the ancestor of the modern, large, one-toed horse.[52] It is now doubtful that Eohippus should have ever been classified in the horse family. Eohippus is probably an extinct type of hyrax.[53]

Evolutionists believe that invertebrates (animals without backbones) have evolved into vertebrates (animals with backbones). However, no transitional form between the two has ever been found.[54]

This lack of transitional forms is very problematic for the evolution model. It has been over 130 years since Darwin wrote *The Origin of Species*. Still, no missing links have been found. Due to this absence of evidence for evolution, modern evolutionists like Stephen Jay Gould have proposed a new model called "Punctuated Equilibrium."[55] Whereas evolution means "gradual change," Punctuated Equilibrium teaches that the changes occurred so suddenly that transitional forms did not survive long enough to be fossilized. It appears that Punctuated Equilibrium is an attempt to explain away the absence of evidence for evolution—but it fails as well.

Since there is no evidence of missing links in the fossil record, evolution should be rejected. The lack of transitional forms in the fossil record is evidence against evolution and in favor of the creation model, which teaches that there are no missing links.[56]

MUTATIONS

Evolutionists need a mechanism that explains how evolution has supposedly occurred. Many evolutionists believe that mutation is this mechanism.[57] However, as was mentioned in the last chapter, mutations merely scramble the already existing genetic code. No new genetic information is added.[58] Yet, for evolution to have occurred, a mechanism is needed through which new genes are produced. Therefore, mutations fail to explain evolution. Evolutionists claim that they believe the present interprets the past. However, there is no mechanism in the present that spontaneously produces new genetic information. Until such a mechanism is found, evolution can only be accepted by "blind faith."

HEISENBERG'S PRINCIPLE
OF INDETERMINACY

Heisenberg's principle of indeterminacy is a theory in quantum physics. Quantum physics deals with the atom and the motion of subatomic particles.[59] The principle of indeterminacy states that it is impossible to determine both the position in space of a subatomic particle and that particle's motion at the same time.[60] Therefore, subatomic particle movement is currently unpredictable for man. This simply means that scientists aren't yet able to accurately predict where a specific particle will be at a given moment. Some scientists have wrongly concluded from this that things can occur on the subatomic level without a cause. If this were true, then it would be possible that the universe just popped into existence without a cause. If this were the case, it would not favor either evolution or creation. If things can come into existence without a cause, then the basis for modern science crumbles. All experiments would be a waste of time, for any given phenomena could have come into existence without a cause. Therefore, there would be no need to study the elements of the universe any longer. Modern science would die.

Albert Einstein believed that Heisenberg's principle did not prove that things can occur without a cause. Einstein held that the causes actually do exist, though man may not be able to find them.[61] Man is limited in knowledge, and there may be some causes he is unable to find.[62] Heisenberg's principle, therefore, cannot come to the aid of evolution; the universe (since it had a beginning) needs a cause.

CONCLUSION

In conclusion, evolution is not a proven fact. It is assumed to be true by many scientists, but they have offered no convincing proofs. There is no evidence for the evolution model. This can be seen in the many unproven assumptions held by evolutionists.

First, there is no evidence for spontaneous generation. The belief that life evolved from non-life contradicts both the cell theory and the law of biogenesis. The Miller-Urey experiments have failed to produce life in the lab (if they were successful, it would be evidence for the creation model not the evolution model).

Second, there is no evidence for the evolutionary assumption that the universe is eternal. Evolutionists must accept this by faith. Evolutionists may assume that the universe evolved into existence from nothing, but this assumption goes against all available scientific evidence as well as logic itself. Nonbeing cannot cause being; from nothing, nothing comes.

Third, there is no evidence that intelligence could come from non-intelligence. Intelligence shows evidence of design; it could not have been produced by chance.

Fourth, no evidence has been found proving that multicelled animals came from single-celled animals. (Even the human embryo does not evolve into a human; it has its full human genetic code at conception.) [63]

Fifth, there is no evidence for the evolution of animals with backbones from animals without backbones.[64] Though there should be multitudes of transitional forms between the two groups, none have been found.

Sixth, there is no evidence for the common ancestry of fish, reptiles, birds, and mammals.[65] Common anatomy could point to a common Designer; it does not necessarily point to common ancestry.

All the major gaps that evolution must cross are assumed to have occurred; they have not been proven to have occurred. Therefore, evolution itself is an unproven assumption. Those who dogmatically proclaim it as truth spend more time explaining away the scientific evidence against their view than they do providing evidence for their view. Any scientific model which lacks plausibility should be abandoned. Such is the case with evolution.

Evolution needs God, but God does not need evolution. If evolution is true, then God is needed to bring the universe into existence from nothing, to bring life from non-life, and complex life forms from simple life forms. In each case, a miraculous superseding of natural laws is needed. However, if God exists, He does not need evolution. He could have either started the long evolutionary process or He could have created the universe in six literal days. God could have used evolution, but if He did, He covered His tracks. He left no evidence. Since God is not the author of deception, it is reasonable to conclude that evolution is a myth.

ENDNOTES

[1] Tom M. Graham, *Biology, the Essential Principles* (Philadelphia: Saunders College Publishing, 1982), 75.

[2] Ibid.

[3] Ibid.

[4] Hugh Ross, *The Fingerprint of God* (Orange: Promise Publishing Company, 1991), 53-105.

[5] Henry M. Morris, *Science and the Bible* (Chicago: Moody Press, 1986), 17.

[6] Ibid., 66.

[7] Ibid.

[8] Morris, *Many Infallible Proofs*, 292-293.

[9] Ibid., 294.

[10] Ibid., 295-296.

[11] Ibid., 296.

[12] Ibid., 295.

[13] Paul D. Ackerman, *It's A Young World After All* (Grand Rapids: Baker Book House, 1986), 72.

[14] Ibid., 73.

[15] Ibid., 74-75.

[16] Hugh Ross, *Creation and Time* (Colorado Springs: NavPress, 1994), 97-99.

[17] Ibid., entire book.

[18] Geisler and Anderson, *Origin Science*, 150-153.

[19] Ibid., 150-152.

[20] Louis Agassiz, "Contribution to the Natural History of the United States," *American Journal of Science*, (1860): 144-145.

[21] Stephen Jay Gould, "Evolution's Erratic Pace," *Natural History*, (May 1977): [14].

[22] Morris, *Science and the Bible*, 67.

[23] Huse, 46.

[24] Ackerman, 83.

[25] Ibid., 84.

[26] Ibid.

27 Ibid.

28 Morris, *Science and the Bible*, 68-69.

29 Ibid.

30 Huse, 147.

31 Morris, *Science and the Bible*, 70.

32 Ibid., 73.

33 Ibid., 74.

34 Ibid., 75.

35 Ibid., 82-85.

36 Ibid., 83.

37 Ibid., 81.

38 Henry M. Morris, *The Biblical Basis for Modern Science* (Grand Rapids: Baker Book House, 1984), 350-359. Some of the recent dinosaur sightings noted by Morris include: smaller brontosaurus in the rain forests of the Congo, living plesiosaurs in the Loch Ness and numerous other waterways, and what appears to be a freshly decayed plesiosaur captured and photographed by Japanese fishermen off the coast of New Zealand.

39 Morris, *Science and the Bible*, 58.

40 Huse, 98.

41 Morris, *Science and the Bible*, 56.

42 Marvin Lubenow, *Bones of Contention* (Grand Rapids: Baker Book House, 1992), 79.

43 Morris, *Science and the Bible*, 56.

44 Ibid.

45 Ibid., 57-58.

46 Lubenow, 167.

47 Morris, *Science and the Bible*, 58.

48 Ibid.

49 Huse, 110.

50 Morris, *Science and the Bible*, 267-268. see also Huse, 110-112.

51 Huse, 112.

52 Morris, *Science and the Bible*, 54-55.

53 Ibid.

54 Huse, 44.

55 Geisler and Anderson, 150-153.

56 Ibid.

57 Morris, *Science and the Bible*, 46-47.

58 Ibid.

59 *The World Book Encyclopedia* (Chicago: World Book, Inc., 1985), vol. 16, 4.

60 Roy E. Peacock, 56-59.

61 Ibid., 59.

62 Moreland, *Scaling the Secular City*, 38-39.

63 Huse, 120.

64 Ibid., 44.

65 Ibid.

CHAPTER 15

The Conclusion

I f God exists, life has meaning. If God exists, there are
such things as right and wrong. There will be life after
death and a future judgment.

Man desperately needs meaning in life, but if there is no
God, then life is absurd and without ultimate meaning. In
Ecclesiastes, Solomon says that a man's life is meaningless
until he recognizes his relation to God. Solomon was not the
only great thinker to argue for the absurdity of life without
God. Blaise Pascal stated that "there are only two classes of
persons who can be called reasonable: those who serve God
with all their heart because they know him and those who
seek him with all their heart because they do not know him."
Jesus said, "Man shall not live on bread alone, but on every
word that proceeds out of the mouth of God" (Matthew 4:4).

Though many people deny or ignore the existence of God,
their lives display a vacuum only He can fill. All people

have a basic need for God. Since all men have a void that only God can fill, this indicates that God exists.

Atheism is the belief that God does not exist. Agnosticism is the belief that man cannot know if God exists. Both of these positions have been shown to be false. Neither one is consistent. Christian Theism has been shown to be the only consistent worldview. Like atheism and agnosticism, pantheism, panentheism, deism, finite godism, polytheism, and skepticism have all been shown to be failures. They are self-contradictory and fail to explain the available evidence.

Strong philosophical arguments have been given for the existence of the God of theism: when combined the cosmological and teleological arguments are quite strong in arguing for God's existence. The moral argument for God's existence is also strong. A person might arbitrarily deny the existence of the moral law, but the denial is forced and temporary. If that person is wronged, he will appeal to the moral law for justice.

One of the greatest obstacles keeping people from accepting Christ is the problem of evil. Is God the cause of evil? Augustine stated that God did not create evil; He merely created the possibility for evil by giving men and angels free will. When men and angels exercised their free will by disobeying God, they actualized the possibility for evil. Therefore, the existence of evil does not disprove the existence of an all-good and all-powerful God. These two are not mutually exclusive.

Not only does God exist, but He is active in the affairs of mankind. A theistic God is a personal God, and a personal God can choose to perform miracles. Some reject miracles because they have a supernatural Cause, but the cosmological argument has shown that the universe itself needs a supernatural Cause. Therefore, since God created the universe, He has no problem intervening in His universe by supernaturally working miracles within it. A person cannot rule out miracles simply because his world view does not allow them.

The absolute moral law is eternal and unchanging. Since the absolute moral law leads directly to the existence of the theistic God, many atheists and pantheists may feel compelled to reject its existence. Also, people who wish to live promiscuous lives often choose to reject God's existence. The apostle John talks about these people when he says:

> And this is the judgment, that the light is come into the world, and men loved the darkness rather than the light; for their deeds were evil. For everyone who does evil hates the light, and does not come to the light, lest his deeds should be exposed (John 3:19-20).

Another argument against God's existence comes from the so-called theory of evolution. But, it has been shown that evolution is not a scientific law or theory, let alone a scientific fact. The second law of thermodynamics and the law of biogenesis militate against the evolutionary hypothesis.

The creation model, which is found in the Bible, is the view that God created the universe without using evolution. The scientific case for creationism is very strong. The principles of analogy and causality support creationism as a superior model to evolution.

Evolution has a fatal flaw. It needs a beginning. For evolution to have occurred, it would need God to start the process. However, God does not need evolution. If evolution is true, then God is needed to bring the universe into existence from nothing, to bring life from non-life, and complex life forms from simple life forms. In each case, a miraculous superseding of natural laws is needed. However, God does not need evolution. God could have used evolution, but if He did, He "covered His tracks" so well that that He left no evidence for it. Thus, we conclude that evolution is a myth, and God sits enthroned.

About the Author

D r. Phil Fernandes is the president of the Institute of Biblical Defense, which he founded in 1990 to teach Christians how to defend the Christian Faith. He is also the pastor of Trinity Bible Fellowship in Bremerton, Washington, and teaches apologetics and philosophy for Columbia Evangelical Seminary and Cascade Bible College. Fernandes has earned the following degrees: a Ph.D. in Philosophy of Religion from Greenwich University, a Master of Arts in Religion from Liberty University, and a Bachelor of Theology from Columbia Evangelical Seminary. Fernandes has publicly debated leading atheists in defense of Christianity at colleges and universities such as Princeton and the University of North Carolina (Chapel Hill). Fernandes is a member of three professional societies: the Evangelical Theological Society, the Evangelical Philosophical Society, and the Society of Christian Philosophers. He has authored several books: *The God Who Sits Enthroned: Evidence for God's Existence, No Other Gods: A Defense of Biblical Christianity, Theism vs. Atheism: The Internet Dabate* (co-authored with leading atheist Dr. Michael Martin), and *God Government, and the Road to Tyranny: A Christian View of Government and Morality.*

Books, videos, and over 400 audio cassette lectures by Dr. Fernandes can be purchased from the Institute of Biblical Defense through the address, phone number, or website listed below:

The Institute of Biblical Defense
P. O. Box 3264
Bremerton, WA 98310

(360) 698-7382
www.biblicaldefense.org

CPSIA information can be obtained
at www.ICGtesting.com
Printed in the USA
FFOW03n0646021217
43802803-42716FF